A LEVER
AND
A **PLACE**
TO
STAND

THE CONTEMPLATIVE STANCE, THE ACTIVE PRAYER

RICHARD ROHR
WITH A FOREWORD BY
JAMES MARTIN, SJ

HiddenSpring

Cover design by Joy Taylor
Book design by Lynn Else
Cover photo: HIP / Art Resource, NY. Ann Ronan Picture Library, London, Great Britain. From the title page of "The Mechanic's Magazine," London, 1824.

Library of Congress Cataloging-in-Publication Data

Rohr, Richard.
　A lever and a place to stand : the contemplative stance, the active prayer / Richard Rohr ; foreword by James Martin.
　　　p. cm.
　Includes bibliographical references (p.　　).
　ISBN 978-1-58768-064-9 (alk. paper)
　1. Contemplation. 2. Christian life—Catholic authors. I. Title.
BV5091.C7R643 2012
248.3′4—dc22

　　　　　　　　　　　　　　　　　　　　　　　　　　　2010040605

Published by
HiddenSpring
An Imprint of Paulist Press
997 Macarthur Boulevard
Mahwah, New Jersey 07430

Printed and bound in the
United States of America

CONTENTS

Starting with their gift of a "Little Portion"
of their land in Assisi to St. Francis,
the Benedictines have always grounded
and blessed the Franciscans.

I very happily dedicate this book
to Fr. John Main, OSB, and Fr. Laurence Freeman, OSB,
for giving me—and our world—much more
than a little portion
of inspiration and encouragement,
many spiritual levers, and some very good places to stand.
We all thank you!

"God makes us ask ourselves questions most often when he intends to resolve them."

—Thomas Merton

FOREWORD

A few years ago, a friend of mine in Catholic publishing asked if I might like to have dinner with Richard Rohr. It was in the middle of a large religious conference in Los Angeles, where many writers and scholars were speaking to colossal crowds of believers and seekers from across the country. "Are you kidding?" I said. "I'd love to." I had long been an admirer of Father Rohr's extraordinary work and had, just that morning, attended one of his standing-room-only talks. His writings and lectures always—*always*—remind me of what those who heard Jesus often said about the surprising carpenter from Galilee: "He speaks with authority." Rohr's straightforward approach to the Christian spiritual life is so obviously based in a deeply contemplative stance that his books often surprise people with insights that seem at once completely new and beautifully old—as if he were helping you discover some wonderful truth that you had somehow forgotten.

But then I wondered, "What if he doesn't live up to my expectations?" After all, I had been reading Rohr's works for years, and had a well-thumbed and heavily underlined copy of his *Everything Belongs* on my bookshelf. How could the man possibly compete with his books and speeches?

What I didn't understand was that someone who had meditated so deeply on the life of Christ, on the Jewish and

Christian scriptures, on the lives of the saints, and, especially, on the story of his beloved St. Francis of Assisi, would be exactly who Richard Rohr turned out to be that night: humble, attentive, insightful, compassionate, and, in a word, alive. What astonished me most about our convivial dinner was how the great man seemed not interested at all in talking about himself, his many books and speaking engagements, or even his marvelous Center for Action and Contemplation, which offers those in social-justice ministries a place for quiet meditation in the sun-bleached scrublands of New Mexico. Rather, he was profoundly interested in the Other, or rather the others—the two people with whom he dined that night, much as I imagine Jesus was always lovingly attentive to those with whom he ate, worked, and prayed.

Richard Rohr's new book *A Lever and a Place to Stand* is, typically, a gem. It is full of the clearheaded and compassionate wisdom that his readers have long expected from this modern spiritual master. The night I met him, Father Rohr surprised me with his humble humanity. May your encounter with him in these pages surprise you with insights and ideas to help you become the person you were meant to be, the person whom God has created.

—Rev. James Martin, SJ, author of
*Becoming Who You Are: Insights on the True Self
from Thomas Merton and Other Saints*

Preface

BRIGHTNESS AND THE HOLY SPIRIT

The Greatest Art Form

"I die by brightness and the Holy Spirit."

—*Thomas Merton*

I dare to call action and contemplation the greatest art form because I believe that it is. It underlies all those other, more visible art forms that we see in great sculpture, music, writing, and painting, and, most especially, in the art form called human character. When these two are one, we always have beauty, symmetry, and transformative form—lives and actions that inherently sparkle and heal, even with dark images.

With most humans, the process begins on the action side. It is surely the first half of life for almost all of us, even introverts. We learn, we experiment, we try, we do, we stumble, we fall, we break, and we find. It is largely done in the outer world of activity, starting with crawling, walking, playing, and speaking. The stage gradually gets larger for these "enactments," but we are still constructing our own good stage on which to act. (We just don't know it yet!)

Yes, there are inner thoughts, feelings, and imaginings during this time. Maybe even sustained study, prayer, or disciplined thought, but do not call that contemplation. These are necessarily and almost always *self-referential*, both for good and for ill. Do not be put off by this, but at this point it is still largely about "me" and finding my own preferred and proper viewing platform. *It has to be*, and it is good. But it is not yet the great, much less the greatest, art form of the union between action and contemplation that we want to talk about here. We must go further.

We can expand because of our actions and reflections, or we can use them to contract. The teaching and guidance that is needed early on is about process more than content. *How* can I see and use my action and my reflections to expand and not to contract? *How* can I listen for God and learn God's *voice*, more than God's precise name and plan. *How* can I keep my heart, mind, and soul open "in hell"?

This should be the early form of spiritual teaching: not *what* to see, nearly as much as *how* to see. I am afraid this cannot usually be taught in book or catechism form; it is picked up largely by "rubbing off" parents and significant others. Could this be the real laying on of hands, the deepest meaning of "apostolic succession"? Could this be the way the Spirit is passed from vessel to vessel? I personally think so.

But if such soul work is learned, usually by osmosis, one will keep growing—and the contemplative side of the soul will begin to show itself. There are already "hints and guesses," as T. S. Eliot would put it, early in the first half of life; and some chosen souls like Thérèse of Lisieux or Gerard Manley Hopkins seem to get the hints and make the guesses. But for most of us, it is a longer process of being drawn by "brightness and the Holy Spirit," as Merton says above. However, note that Merton says he "dies" by this brightness, because, although we are pulled into the

Mystery through our actions and beyond our actions in the first half of life, it will be felt and experienced as a kind of dying and yet a dying into what always feels bigger and brighter. But first of all, contemplation is a series of losses, largely our illusions. If the early process of *"how"* did not go deep, we will use all incoming data (read, "actions") to defend ourselves, protect ourselves from our shadow, and build a leaden manhole cover over our unconscious. We will settle for being right instead of being holy and whole; for saying prayers instead of being one.

Remember, the ego wants containment and control. It is only the soul that wants meaning and mystery. In fact, that is how you can tell the difference between whether it is your ego that is leading you—or "brightness and the Holy Spirit"! If I have not found a way to hear and allow that deeper level of soul, I will use all my roles, my relationships, and even my religion to fortify my ego and my private agenda. I might even say a lot of prayers, but it will not be the spacious world of contemplation. It will be dualistic and will involve drawn-out devotions, always needing another one because the past one did not work. The "big field" has not yet opened up. The "brightness" has not happened.

Remember, Jesus said, "When you pray, do not keep on babbling like the pagans" (Matt 6:7; NIV).

Contemplation waits for the moments, creates the moments, where all can be a prayer. It refuses the very distinction between action and contemplation. Contemplation is essentially nondual consciousness that overcomes the gaps between me and God, outer and inner, either and or, me and you (see Richard Rohr, *The Naked Now: Learning to See as the Mystics See*, New York: Crossroad, 2008).

The reason why the true contemplative-in-action is still somewhat rare is that most of us, even and most especially in religion, have gained a PhD in dualistic thinking. And then we try to use such a limited tool for prayer, problem, or relationship. It cannot and will not get us very far.

We are led forward by brightness and by that I mean a "larger force field" that includes the negative, the problematic, the difficult, the unknown—that which I do not yet understand, the Mysterious that God always is. Brightness is not into exclusion or denial of anything.

The irony of ego "consciousness" is that it always excludes and eliminates the unconscious—so it is actually not conscious at all! It insists on knowing, of being certain, and it refuses all unknowing. So most people who think they are fully conscious (read, "smart") have that big leaden manhole cover over their unconscious. It gives them control but seldom compassion or wisdom. That is exactly why politicians, priests, and CEOs of anything will predictably continue to fail and fall as the Inner Mystery continues to show itself through them and to them.

The beauty of the unconscious is that it knows a great deal, whether personal or collective, but it always knows that it does not know, cannot say, dare not try to prove or assert too strongly, because what it *does* know is that there is *always more—and all words will fall short*. The contemplative is precisely the person who agrees to live in that kind of brightness. The paradox, of course, is that it does not feel like brightness at all, but what John of the Cross calls a "luminous darkness," or others call "learned ignorance." In summary, you cannot grow in the great art form, the integration of action and contemplation, without 1) a strong tolerance for ambiguity; 2) an ability to allow, forgive, and contain a certain degree of anxiety; and 3) a willingness to not know and not even need to know. This is how you allow and encounter Mystery. All else is mere religion.

Finally, of course, one can do this only if Someone Else is holding you during such dying. If Someone Else is taking away your fear. If Someone Else is doing the knowing. If Someone Else is a really great and satisfying Lover! If you can allow that Someone Else to have their way with you, you will go back to your life of action with new vitality, but it will now be smooth, One Flow. It will be "no longer you" who acts or contemplates, but the life of One who lives in you (Gal 2:20), now acting for you and with you, and *as you*! Henceforth, it does not even matter whether you act *or* contemplate, contemplate or act, because both will be inside the One Flow that is still and forever loving and healing the world. This is how you "die by brightness and the Holy Spirit." This is the greatest art form.

ACKNOWLEDGMENTS

Grateful acknowledgment is made to the John Main Seminar at the World Community for Christian Meditation, based in London, where the present work by Fr. Richard Rohr, OFM, began as a part of the John Main Seminar. The seminar is a major annual event of the World Community for Christian Meditation, which brings members together from around the world and is open to all. A prominent teacher or public figure leads the seminar.

About the World Community for Christian Meditation

The World Community for Christian Meditation took form in 1991. It continues John Main's legacy in teaching Christian meditation and his work of restoring the contemplative dimension of Christian faith in the life of the church. This began with his opening of the first center for teaching Christian meditation in London in 1975

The Community is now directed by Laurence Freeman, OSB, a student of John Main, and a Benedictine monk of the Olivetan Congregation. The World Community has its international center and a retreat center in London. There are a number of centers in other parts of the world. The Community is thus a "monastery without walls," a family of national communities and emerging communities in over a hundred countries. The foundation of the Community is the local meditation group, which meets weekly in homes, parishes, offices, hospitals, prisons, and colleges. The World Community also works closely with many Christian churches.

The Community runs the annual John Main Seminar and the Way of Peace. It also sponsors retreats, training schools for teachers of meditation seminars, lectures, and other programs. It contributes to interfaith dialogues particularly, in recent years, with Buddhists and Muslims. A quarterly spiritual letter with news of the Community is mailed and is also available online. Weekly readings can be sent directly by e-mail. Information on current programs, connections to national coordinators, and the location of meditation groups can all be found on the Community Web site at www.wccm.org, which also offers a range of online audio talks and videos. This site is the hub of a growing family of Internet presence, the Web sites of national communities, and special interests, such as the teaching of meditation to children, the eleventh step of twelve-step recovery programs, and the spirituality of priests.

Medio Media is the communication and publishing arm of the World Community and offers a wide range of books, audios, and videos to support the practice of meditation. The online bookstore is at www.mediomedia.com.

Topics and speakers of past John Main Seminars include—

2009   Robert Kennedy, SJ: "When God Disappears"
2008   Cardinal Walter Kasper: "Unity: Local and Global"

2007   Charles Taylor, Laurence Freeman, Balfour Mount, Sarah Bachelard, and Peter Ng: "Still Present: The Life and Legacy of John Main"

2006   Margaret Rizza: "The Fire of Silence through Music and Mystics"

2005   Richard Rohr, OFM: "A Lever and a Place to Stand"

2004   Joan Chittister, OSB: "Heart of Flesh: A Feminist Spirituality for Women and Men"

2003   Andrew Harvey, Shirley du Boulay, and Bruno Barnhart, OSB Cam: "Bede Griffiths, OSB"

2002   Bishop Kallistos Ware: "The Kingdom of the Heart: The Jesus Prayer in Our Daily Life"

2001   Archbishop Rowan Williams: "Spirit in the Desert"

2000   The Dalai Lama and Previous Presenters: "The Way of Peace"

1999   Huston Smith: "Return to the Light"

1998   Thomas Keating, OCSO: "Heart of the World"

1997   Mary McAleese: "Reconciled Being"

1996   Raimon Panikkar: "The Silence of Life"

1995   Laurence Freeman, OSB: "On Jesus"

1994   The Dalai Lama: "The Good Heart"

1993   William Johnston, SJ: "The New Christian Mysticism"

1992   Jean Vanier: "From Brokenness to Wholeness"

1991   Bede Griffiths, OSB: "Christian Meditation: An Evolving Tradition"

1990   Eileen O'Hea, CSJ: "Spirit and Psyche"

1989   Balfour Mount: "On Wholeness"

1988   Charles Taylor: "Christian Identity and Modernity"

1987   Derek Smith: "On Reading"

Chapter One

A LEVER AND A PLACE TO STAND

"Give me a lever and a place to stand and I will move the world."

—*Archimedes*

Archimedes (c. 287–c. 212 BC) was a Greek philosopher and mathematician. He noticed that if a lever was balanced in the right place, on the right fulcrum, it could move proportionally much greater weights than the force actually applied. Archimedes wanted a fixed point in space. If the earth was balanced on one end of a lever, when Archimedes applied his weight on the other side, it was magnified by the distance from the fulcrum. Therefore, if the earth was distance x from the fixed point, and Archimedes was jumping up and down on the other end of a lever that was one million times x in length, then his small weight would be magnified a million times and the earth theoretically could be moved. If the lever stretched far enough *and the fulcrum point remained fixed close to the earth*, then even a small weight at one end would be able to move the world at the other. I think this offers us a fine metaphor for what I want to say about contemplation and action in this book.

The fixed point is our place to stand. It is a contemplative stance: steady, centered, poised, and rooted. To be

1

contemplative, we have to have a slight distance from the world—we have to allow time for withdrawal from business as usual, for meditation, for prayer in what Jesus calls "our private room." However, in order for this not to become escapism, we have to remain quite close to the world at the same time, loving it, feeling its pains and its joys as *our* pains and *our* joys. So the fulcrum must be somehow be in the real world. True contemplation, all the great masters say, is really quite down to earth and practical, and does not require life in a monastery. It is just an utterly different way of receiving the moment, from all of life and from anywhere. However, in order to have the capacity to "move the world," we ironically need some distancing and detachment from the diversionary nature of mass culture, useless distractions, and the daily delusions of the false self. (See "True Self / False Self," a recorded conference available through the Center for Action and Contemplation in Albuquerque, New Mexico, www.cacradicalgrace.org.) Contemplation builds on the hard bottom of reality—as it is—without ideology, denial, or fantasy.

St. Francis of Assisi and Thomas Merton continue to have a huge historic impact—even though just individuals—because each one's vision was at the same time both radically critical of consumer culture and also in love with the world. They overcame the seeming tension and found underneath what I will call here the Unified Field. Thomas Merton called it "a hidden wholeness," and Francis sang of it in his famous "Canticle of Brother Sun," which has become the de facto theme song of Christian ecology.

So I am using Archimedes' discovery on a different level—allegorically, as the church fathers would say. What strikes me is that we don't have a fixed place to stand, a fulcrum of critical distance, and thus many of us cannot find our levers, or true "delivery systems," by which to move our world. We do not have the steadiness of spiritual practice to keep our sight keen and alive. Those who have the opportunity for spiritual practice—for example, those in monasteries—often don't have an access point from which to speak to or serve much of our world. We don't usually have a delivery system in the world beyond religion itself, which weakens our capacity for building bridges and connecting the dots of life.

Some degree of inner experience is necessary for true spiritual authority, but finally we need some form of outer validation too. We need to be taken seriously as competent and committed individuals, and not just "inner" people. Could this perhaps be what Jesus means by being both "wise as serpents and innocent as doves?" (Matt 10:16). I personally think that is what the aphorism is describing. God offers us quiet contemplative eyes, but God also calls us to prophetic and critical involvement in the pain and sufferings of our world—at the same time. That is so obvious in the life and ministry of Jesus that one wonders why it would even be questioned.

When you are lacking in any inner experience of God, grace, and inner movements of life and love, you will lack any real spiritual authority. People can tell the difference today. Mere titles or ordination no longer suffice, but actual inner experience and inner authority are what people demand and deserve in our time. Remember, Jesus himself was neither a rabbi, nor a trained teacher of the Law. He was a layman who knew God and God's ways; the Twelve that he chose were apparently the same—after his training at least.

Today people know when we are just quoting clichés that we hardly believe ourselves, mouthing doctrines that have no real grounding within us, and offering teachings that are mere textbook answers. This innate wisdom of good people is rightly called by the church the *sensus fidelium*, a certain Christian common sense and deep intuition that can taste, smell, and touch the real spirit of God and Jesus (1 John 1:1) and distinguish it from what is bogus or immature. The issues are too global and too urgent today to settle for anything less. Contemplation, perhaps like nothing else, establishes you inside the *sensus fidelium* of the Unified Field of the Holy Spirit.

Fortunately, the classic Christian polarities of action and contemplation always feed, regulate, balance, and integrate one another. To even know good, *you have to do something first*! This is why I intentionally put the word *action* before the word *contemplation* in the naming of our Center in Albuquerque, New Mexico. But the very limitations and failures of your "doing" will drive you back and deeper into contemplation. And so the cycle of life and prayer begins. After a while you are never sure which is feeding which, or whether it is action or contemplation that comes first. They live through one another, and neither of them by themselves. But finally you will have both your lever and your place to stand—and from there, you can move your bit of the world, because you are being moved yourself inside a much larger Flow.

Chapter Two

AMUSING OURSELVES TO DEATH

I want to begin with a rather extended quotation from a book that was written in 1985 by Neil Postman and that continues to sell very well after twenty-five years: *Amusing Ourselves to Death: Public Discourse in the Age of Show Business* (New York: Penguin Books). What Postman does in this book is point out that modern education, journalism, religion, and almost all public discourse have largely taken the form of entertainment. According to his understanding, Americans are indeed "entertaining themselves to death."

He begins the book in this way:

> We were keeping our eye on 1984. The year came and the prophesy didn't. Thoughtful Americans sang softly in praise of themselves. The roots of liberal democracy had held. Wherever else the terror had happened, we, at least, had not been visited by Orwellian nightmares.
>
> But we had forgotten that alongside Orwell's dark vision, there was another—slightly older, slightly less well known, equally chilling: Aldous Huxley's *Brave New World*. Contrary to common belief even among the educated, Huxley and Orwell did not prophesy the same thing. Orwell

5

warns that we will be overcome by an externally imposed oppression. But in Huxley's vision, no Big Brother is required to deprive people of their autonomy, maturity and history. As he saw it, people will come to love their oppression, to adore the technologies that undo their very capacity to think.

What Orwell feared were those who would ban books. What Huxley feared was that there would be no reason to ban a book, for there would be no one who wanted to read one. Orwell feared those who would deprive us of information. Huxley feared those who would give us so much that we would be reduced to passivity and egoism. Orwell feared that the truth would be concealed from us. Huxley feared the truth would be drowned in a sea of irrelevance. Orwell feared we would be become a captive culture. Huxley feared we would become a trivial culture, preoccupied with some equivalent of the feelies, the orgy porgy, and the centrifugal bumble-poppy [Huxley's names for the drug, sex, and technological diversions in his novel]. As Huxley remarked in *Brave New World Revisited*, the civil libertarians and rationalists who are ever on the alert to oppose tyranny "failed to take into account man's almost infinite appetite for distraction." In *1984*, Huxley added, people are controlled by inflicting pain. In *Brave New World*, they are controlled by inflicting pleasure. In short, Orwell feared that what we hate will ruin us. Huxley feared that what we love will ruin us. (vii–viii)

Neil Postman writes a book about the possibility that Huxley in fact was right, and Orwell largely missed the point. This lays a foundation for what I want to affirm in this book: the importance of an inner life, a life that is grounded in contemplation, a life that searches for the hidden wholeness underneath the passing phenomena, a life that seeks substance instead of simply an endless preoccupation with forms.

The West—and America, in particular—are fascinated with forms. We like impermanent things, maybe because they can't nail us down to anything solid or lasting, and we float in an ephemeral and transient world of argumentative ideas. It's not bearing a lot of fruit. It seems to me that it is creating people who are very unsure of themselves and who seem to be grasping in every direction for a momentary sense of identity, for a momentary sense of importance. We see this especially in our young people.

Charles Peguy, the tormented French poet, said with great insight that "everything worthwhile begins in mysticism and ends in politics" (Marjorie Villiers, *Charles Peguy: A Study in Integrity*, Harper, 1965). Everything worthwhile puts together the two things that don't look like they are together at all, but always have been at a deeper level. The goal is to get people to that deeper level, to the Unified Field, or what I like to call nondual thinking, where God alone can hold the contradictions together.

When people ask me which is the more important, action or contemplation, I know it is an impossible question because they are eternally united in one embrace, two sides of one coin. So I say that *action* is not the important word, *contemplation* is not the important word: *AND* is the important word! How do you put the action and contemplation together perfectly? I am sixty-seven now and I'm still working on it! It certainly is the great art form, as I said in the preface. To begin with a mystical moment and to end in what looks like politics is the norm, as far as I can see. This is the great dance that we work toward in Christian spirituality.

Recently I have made a more serious study of the works of John Main. In the past, I had looked at him in a cursory way; he was one good teacher among many teachers, but when I had to really take him seriously, I was never disappointed. He is a writer who doesn't say things in flashy ways. If I were in a superficial mode, I wouldn't be too impressed, but if in a more centered and grounded place, I would again and again say, "He's right, he's right!" John Main is a great teacher of the necessary fixed point, the place to stand, which for him was the stability of the mantra and the daily practice of twice-daily formal meditation.

At the same time, I find John Main helpful as a teacher of the dance of contemplation and action. He is a prophet but not in an obvious way. He is a prophet more in what he does *not* say: he doesn't talk directly about social issues or about current political issues. Instead, he draws our attention away from the "issues" that entertain us and reveals to us our basic distraction and superficiality. Prophets see the depths of things; our greatest sin, perhaps, is that we live on the periphery of things. John Main speaks from a place of critical distance from the illusions of this world, and in that way his words have weight and substance. His teachings, like that of other great contemplatives like Thomas Merton and my father St. Francis, *do* have the power to move the world.

I'm lucky as a Franciscan to do my Lent in a hermitage every other year. During that time, I am cut off from the news, and I'm struck on my return how I haven't missed anything, how nothing at all was necessary to know. As Neil Postman says, you realize news is largely manufactured to fill up the half hour and to make you feel it is monumental or important. In fact, there is, as John Main says, really only "one mystery, one truth, one suffering, one love, one life, and it is just showing itself in different forms." He calls it "the universal consciousness of the Risen Christ" that holds this great picture of life together. Augustine, of course, called this creative holding of both death and resurrection at the same time the paschal mystery, the place where all transformation happens, the liminal space where God is in charge for a while.

I used to give a regular talk to incoming interns at our Center to try to establish in their minds this essential link between action and contemplation. It was good to begin with Exodus 3, the story of the burning bush. Moses' experience is surely an inner experience, but mirrored outwardly too. It is a transcendent experience, but one that is significantly based in nature and not in a synagogue or temple. Often it is in the open spaces of the natural world that the inner world is most obviously recognized, as the desert fathers and mothers, and Celtic Christianity, remind us. But within three sentences, after Moses has had his heart-stopping experience, Yahweh says to him: "I have observed the misery of my people who are in Egypt" (Exod 3:7). God doesn't let Moses float around inside his inner experience. He gives it *immediate* focus, implication, and direction. And in this case, it is entirely social and political. So anybody who says liberation theology is new and dangerous does not know how our whole story began.

In recent years, I have been teaching on the spirituality of the Twelve Steps of Alcoholics Anonymous. Its connection with the Gospel is, I think, profound. Bill Wilson's Twelfth Step, which he was very insistent on, told the alcoholics in that early period that they would never really come to appropriate the power and importance of the first Eleven Steps until and unless they personally took it upon themselves to give it away to at least one other person. That is an essential hook that Christians have released themselves from, and have suffered because of it. I am convinced that, in taking away the need and desire to serve and to pay back, a large percentage of Christians lose whatever they might gain in their private devotions.

I know in many ways that, if I have grown at all in my forty years as a priest, it's in part through this role of being a preacher and teacher. I have had to stand before crowds for forty years and describe what I thought I believed, and then I often had to ask myself, "Do I really believe that myself?" And in my attempt to communicate it, I usually found that I'd only scratched the surface of understanding. There is some truth that in sharing, in handing anything over, in giving it away, you really, maybe for the first time, appropriated it yourself as something more and something better than you yourself might have imagined.

Maybe it is because *this Substantial Mystery is a mystery of participation and never of private ownership.* Maybe that is why, alongside trying to be faithful to our individual daily prayer and daily meditation, we also commit ourselves to meditating in groups, almost as if to recognize that whatever has happened is not happening in just me, but it is happening in us together. The One Spirit is held communally. It is important to experience Spirit that way, or we can easily become ego-inflated, thinking that *I* am so contemplative. The goal is to lessen the fortress of *I*, not strengthen the *I* in any apartness or superiority. There is a deep symbiosis in the Body of Christ between the one who thinks he or she is giving and the one who thinks he or she is receiving. The obvious is very often completely reversed.

It seems to me that meditation, as John Main taught it, makes it almost inevitable that your politics is going to change, your time usage is going to be called into question, your snug socioeconomic prospective will be slowly taken away from you. First of all, what happens when anyone regularly meditates is that the things we think of as our necessary ego boundaries—giving us a sense of our independence, our autonomy, our private self-importance—these well-fortified boundaries, fall away, little by little, as unnecessary and even unhelpful. This imperial *I*, this self that the West thinks is the *only* self, is not substantial or lasting at all. It is largely a creation of our own minds. Protecting this *relative identity*, which today we call a *persona* ("mask"), eventually becomes a boring concern. "Why would I bother with that?" the True Self says.

When I went through the teaching of John Main, he says again and again that it's all about living right here, right now. But like Eckhart Tolle, John Main reminds us that the mind is *incapable* of living in the now. The present moment is always boring, and we always hope that the next minute will be better (liberals), or that nostalgia for the past is somehow the truth (conservatives). The mind can do many things but it cannot be in the present. The mind can only rehash the past and worry about the future, or "worry about many things," as Jesus tells Martha, but the mind cannot be present here and now.

The Mystery of Presence

That is why the doctrine of the Real Presence in the Eucharist is so important and why we Catholics defend it. It is the touchstone of orthodoxy, the central sacrament for the journey itself. If you deny that the spiritual cannot enter the material world, then you are in trouble, since we hope to be just that! The incarnation was just once, but not forever, nor in me. We had best encounter incarnation in one focused, dramatic moment, and then the particular truth has a chance of becoming a universal truth. We eat what we are until we know who we are, you might say. That is just good nutrition—that you become what you eat.

But after defending and believing that for all my life, I recognize that the concept of presence is inherently and necessarily relational. Catholics can defend the doctrine of the Real Presence all we want, and I do, but if we don't teach the children of God *how to be present to presence, there is no* Real *Presence.* We Catholics tend to spend much of our time defending the objective end of doctrines and very often we neglect the subjective end—which is where everybody actually lives. If we had spent as much time teaching people *how to be present,* I think we would have had a lot more believers in the Real Presence, and we would have had far less church division over what became merely a heady and irrational belief. Because people had not been taught how to be present themselves, the last five hundred years became futile rational arguments about transubstantiation—the *how,* the *if,* and the *who could do it*—because Encounter itself was no longer the heart of the matter. Presence is only known by presence itself, not by ideating or figuring it out. Anyone who has had even one great moment of human love knows this to be true.

And so what happens in mediation is that we move beyond doctrines and dogmas to inner experience. When we move to the level of experience, we see that this self, which is only a "radio receiver," is not to be taken too seriously, for it is always changing stations and is filled with static and interference. Someone who is faithful to meditation quickly overcomes the illusion that my *correct* thinking, or thinking more about something, can ever get me there. If so, every good PhD would be a saint. You see, *information is not the same as transformation.* Even good and correct thinking is always trapped inside my little mind, my particular culture, my form of education, my parental conditioning— all of which is good and all of which is bad. That places all great mysteries inside my little world, and so we should rightfully be much more humble about our own opinions and thoughts. After all, *how could the Infinite ever be fully or rightly received by the finite?*

Alongside all our knowing, accompanying every bit of our knowing, must be the humble "knowing that we do not know." That's why the great tradition of prayer was balanced by both the *cataphatic,* knowing through images and words, and the *apophatic,* knowing through silence, beyond words; knowing by the empty spaces around the words; knowing by allowing God to fill in all the gaps in an "unspeakable" way. This latter, more mystical way was almost lost in the West after the dualistic conflicts of the Reformation and the headiness of the Enlightenment. It became impossible afterward to have any appreciation for the freedom of not knowing and the spaciousness of not even needing to know! We needed to be certain about everything, because now there were enemies on all sides.

Strangely enough, this unknowing is a new kind of knowing. We have a word for it: *faith,* a kind of knowing that doesn't need to know and yet doesn't dismiss either, a kind of knowing that *doesn't need to hold everything itself because at a deeper level it knows it is being held.* As Paul puts it, "For now we see in a mirror, dimly, but then we will see face to face. Now I know only in part; then I will know fully, even as I have been fully known" (1 Cor 13:12). It took me years to understand this, even though this is straight Franciscan teaching: my mind alone could not get me there. Prayer in my later years has become simply letting myself be nakedly known, as I am, in all my ordinariness, face to face, without any masks or even religious makeup. Such nakedness is a falling into the Unified Field, where you know in a different way and from a different Source. This is another access point: knowing by union, an intuitive grasp of a kind of wholeness, but a truth beyond words, beyond any need or capacity to prove anything right or wrong, which we will call here a contemplative stance toward life, and which is surely our solid place to stand.

Chapter Three

LIVING WITH PARADOX

When I was a young man I had always liked ideas and books, and I remember going into book stores and praying to the Holy Spirit: "Okay, which is the right book that I should read?" Now, when I come back from a longer hermitage, I always have no desire to read a book whatsoever for the next few weeks or even months, and then it gradually wears off. For a while, I know there is nothing in any book that is going to be better, more truthful, or more solid than what I just experienced on the soul and cellular level. Now if you asked me what it is that I know, I would be hard pressed to tell you. All I know is that there is a deep "okayness" to life, despite all the contradictions—which become even more evident in the silence. Even when much is terrible, seemingly contradictory, unjust, and inconsistent, somehow sadness and joy are able to coexist at the same time within you. *The negative valence of things no longer cancels out the positive valence, nor does the positive deny the negative.* It feels like a new way of knowing, living, and seeing.

Whatever your call, your lever, your delivery system for the world—it must proceed from this foundational *yes* to life. Your necessary *no* to injustice and all forms of un-love will actually become even more clear and more urgent in the silence, but now your work has a chance of being God's pure

15

healing instead of your impure anger and agenda. You can always feel the difference in people who are working for causes; so many works of social justice have been undone by people who do all the fighting from their small or angry selves. As indicated in the story of Gideon (Jdgs 7:2–8), Yahweh had to lessen, or even stop, his compulsive *drive*, so the wind of the Spirit could *draw* him more gently and more effectively. This is a major and important shift.

Any true contemplation or meditation gradually overcomes our autonomous and success-driven ego. It slowly undoes any illusion that my cracked thinking can get me out of this inexplicable world. It overcomes that shapeless anxiety that comes from the inherent mystery of life and all my attempts at evasion. That is why your politics, time usage, and economics will always change. If it doesn't, I doubt if your prayer is invading your unconscious. If it does, your whole view of the world will change from fear to connection because you don't live inside your fragile and encapsulated self anymore. You are moving from ego consciousness to soul awareness, from being driven to being drawn.

We have got to admit, no matter where you were in the latest general elections or in the American healthcare debate, that the tenor of public discourse is often infantile—in this country with so many schools and universities. Many of our people know of no other way of thinking. No one told them about the wonderful alternative, a third way beyond fight or flight, which means we have not been offering the Gospel at any depth.

Huxley said there are two prerequisites for a culture of entertainment: First, you shall have no expectations before or filters afterward. Every television program must be a complete package in itself; no previous knowledge is required. There must not be even a hint of learning in any direction. This is an edifice that I can construct together with the news anchor in the next thirty minutes and then come to my own conclusions, although they are usually his. No further reading, study, prayer, or conversation is required. I can even put out my own blog or Web site, asserting things to be true or false without the least foundation or validation. Now, precisely because this mode of thinking is so fragile, that's probably why we wrap ourselves around it so tightly. We have our new cliché, our new opinion, our new conclusion, and that settles all the dust. And we don't like dust; it all must be clean, clear, and concluded.

Second, you shall induce no perplexity in your audience. Perplexity is a super-highway to low ratings in America, and that has been statistically proven many times over. A perplexed listener is a listener who will turn to another station. This means that there must be nothing that has to be remembered, studied, applied, endured, or checked out. We are willing, like blank slates, to believe the loudest voice, or receive the latest poll, or take in whatever else is being said with conviction and authority. When people have no appropriate filters, culture is at the whim of demagogues and sound bites. Education should be the creating of good and helpful filters.

Years ago I did a study on Luke's Gospel, and as I went through the text, I discovered that almost ever time the word *crowd* is used, the crowd is almost always wrong. Mass consciousness, it seems, is never deep or truthful. Mass consciousness cannot hold truth because human truth is always a coincidence of opposites. Take this as normative and even important: *Any life without conflicts is by necessity only half a life*. A certain degree of stress is good and necessary, and shows you are inside the true Mystery.

Full human life demands some shadowboxing with the shadow side of every reality. If we are not willing to do that, if we just want the Republicans or the Democrats to be totally right or America to be perfect, then we are incapable of depth or truth. When everything becomes a secure "belonging" system instead of a transformational experience, people simply localize themselves inside their little world of shared beliefs, and there the fragile self quickly takes on some sense of identity and power: "I'm not very smart myself, but we Catholics as a group are old, big, and smart," or, "I don't know how we could be oppressing the world. America has always been on the side of justice and truth." So we slide inside our collective identities precisely because we have not found a personal identity, to discover who we are, as Paul says, "hidden with Christ in God" (Col 3:3). Before we meet our own soul, most identities are socially mediated; once we find the inner spring of ourselves and the Holy Spirit, we finally begin to be who we really are. Usually that does not happen till the second half of life; but for many, never.

Remember every viewpoint is a view from a point. Now if the point from which you view life is simply my little Richard Rohr self—my American, male, educated, Catholic self—I've got to promote and defend such a little identity. I've got to make sure my viewpoint is the best and is always right. I've always said I was totally prepared for this work because I grew up in Kansas. I was right in the middle of the good old U.S.A., surrounded with an excess of certitudes about everything. I was not only in the best country in the world, but probably the best State, this side of the *Wizard of Oz*. We were either Methodists or Catholics, good upstanding citizens, sharing the same prejudices, but not much crime in those days. I didn't know what divorce or abuse was. Not only was I born in the best country in the world, but I was "one holy Catholic and apostolic" besides. We were Roman Catholics. I can never remember an anti-Protestant sermon; we never put down the Protestants. We just felt sorry for them. We thought their churches were so ugly. "Why would anyone want to go to a Protestant church? They have no imagination or creativity," we thought. We were only half right, of course. And the Protestants were half right.

Obviously we have influenced one another since then! Oh, but *we* were "the one true Church." We were going to Heaven. Then we discovered that most other religions believed the same thing. This is called "group narcissism." There is only one thing more dangerous than individual egocentricity and that is group egocentricity. This happens when the group together agrees upon the same viewpoint, and because the agreement is so total, because no questioning is allowed, it passes for Great Truth. There is great comfort and blindness in such company. Remember, the happy Palm Sunday crowd and the angry Good Friday crowd are largely the same people.

Now don't be surprised by this pattern today because that is exactly what Israel did too. Remember that Judaism is an archetypical religion. Judaism did everything absolutely right and absolutely wrong—just like Catholicism and just like Protestantism—which we will always do until we experience Substantial Reality. It is religion at the beginning stages, preparing us for Encounter Itself. But at that stage we fall in love with forms. We will promote clichés and external doctrines and dogmas as if they were what Martin Heidegger called "the thing in itself." We do not know the thing in itself yet, so we worship the shell. When you have not yet experienced the thing in itself, what else can you fall in love with, except forms, flags, boundary markers, and symbols of loyalty? That's what all early stage religion looks like, swaying "like reeds in the wind," as Jesus would put it. These are not bad people at all. They just have not yet fallen into the hands of a living and loving God.

So until the illusions are taken away from us by some form of inner journey, the mind will always remain dualistic, eliminating anything problematic or mysterious. Until there is inner experience (which we are calling meditation or contemplation), then we can only think in terms of winners and losers. The mind can't even get energy or motivation without comparison: I and you, us and them. We try to convince ourselves that we are alive by winning, and we push ourselves to achieve in all kinds of self-created win/lose situations.

I do a lot of men's spiritual work and this is especially the case with us males. We get energy as soon as there is a team to beat, a race to run, or an army to fight. Take that away from us and there is a palpable loss of interest in what is happening. If we cannot define a cause in terms of good guys and bad guys, then we actually lose our motivation. It is your dualistic mind that will be taken from you in meditation, so be forewarned if you want to hold onto that. Afterward, you will find yourself thinking much more in terms of both/and rather than either/or. That is what enables mystics and saints to forgive, to let go of hurts, to be compassionate, and even to love enemies.

In fact, you cannot do any of the above with a dualistic mind. That's why almost all great spiritual teachers tell us in one form or another, "Do not judge," as Jesus also tells us in several places (e.g., Matt 7:1). The judging mind *is* the dualistic mind. It is always comparing and competing. Men tend to compete more, women tend to compare more, but it is the same ego game. And unfortunately, the comparing and competing soon justify condemning and then even crucifying the other. It is the normal way that the dualistic mind works: one side is invariably judged up and the other is invariably judged down.

But are thought and judgment necessary? Of course they are at certain levels. Still, it took me a long time to recognize that my need to judge was not really a desire for truth as I had convinced myself. My need to judge was a desire for control: To be in control of the data, to be right. To be in control of the explanations, to define the pecking order. To know who's up and who's down. Who is in and who is out. Who is right and who is wrong. Who is superior and who is inferior. That's what is taken away from you and that's why many will never go on the inner journey. Who wants that power to be taken from you? It gives us some kind of comfort to feel superior and secure; momentary comfort that *I am right* takes away our anxiety. Don't believe me? Watch your own behavior. Control is the first need of the ego. (By the way, if you do not like the psychological term *ego*, I am convinced that Paul is pointing to much the same thing with his word *flesh*, but that word has had an even more unfortunate history, since people thought he meant "embodiment.")

The ego defines itself by negation and by contraction: "I'm not that. I am not like her. I am not a sinner. I am not a communist. I am not a heretic." When we have not met our True Self, or what we *are*, we are content with what we are *not*. What we are *not* demands nothing of us whatsoever except putting someone else down, which is supposed to pull *us* up! The sad thing is that it works, and so people keep doing it. I think history will continue to do it until, and unless, we find a place to stand, a contemplative stance. Until we find the totally secure True Self, the false self will always need to win, be right, and, if possible, to defeat the other.

The ego defines itself by contracting, pulling itself in, saying *no*, and/or being against; the soul, however, defines itself by expanding, by including—not by saying *no*, but by offering a kind of courageous, risky *yes*. "Yes, I am like everybody else, capable of the same good and the same bad. They are all my brothers and sisters. The soul knows that we are all equally naked underneath our clothes." Can you feel the scariness in that? When you allow the face of the other, the opinion of the other, the worldview of the other, to break through your barriers and you let down the boundaries, there is always a bit of fear, like in first moments of intimacy.

I can see why Jesus said: "For the gate is narrow and the road is hard that leads to life, and there are few who find it" (Matt 7:14). He is talking first of all about life in this world. On the unconscious level, we know that *true intimacy with anything is going to change us*. And if there is one thing that the ego hates more than anything else, it is to change. We eventually know that if I keep doing this meditation, it is going to change my worldview, my priorities, and my preferences. It will be a new world, and we are hunkered down in this old one. It is a wonder that anyone continues the dangerous journey of prayer, which is, by the way, a step-by-step walk into divine intimacy and soul intimacy at the same time.

Once a radical "justification" has taken place (which is Paul's term for this phenomenon of transformation)—a radical legitimation of the self in God—we are made one, and in a certain sense whole/holy in this world. No wonder it was called "salvation." Then the blind parts of ourselves, the lesser loyalties, take on less and less importance. What meditation does is ground us in a preexistent wholeness that we call Christ Consciousness (e.g., 1 Cor 2:16), so that we will not identify too much or too long with the mere parts and partialities that make such needless divisions in our world and in ourselves.

If you have identified with the parts for forty years, identified with the shadow self, the superior self, any passing loyalty system, it's pretty risky to have these taken away from you. If your whole identity is being a Republican or a Democrat, you had better not pray, you really better not, because your Republican/Democrat identity just isn't going to mean a great deal. Nor will your black/white, gay/straight, rich/poor, American/Asian, or even Christian/non-Christian identity be your rallying cry. You are an utterly new creation, and finally "Christ is all and in all" (Col 3:11; cf. 2 Cor 5:17 and Gal 3:28, if you think this is my idea).

Lesser Loyalties and Father Hunger

I don't think Jesus ever saw the American flag. I very much doubt if he would salute it, or any flag of any other piece of God's One Grand Real Estate, which he called the *"kingdom of God"* or the *"reign of God."* Do not talk this way, however, in polite religious company, or suddenly you're going to have "no place to lay your head" and "the whole world will hate you." Why? Because you are not on either side of the usual categories, the usual loyalty systems and groups where the ego wants to be, to give itself a foundation and a security that it does not actually have.

So all we can do is to go to another place for our foundation and security. As many other teachers have said, once you say, "Jesus is Lord," then, of course, the logical consequence is that no one else is. Yet history has been formed by "Christian" loyalties to the lords of this earth, whoever they might be in their six-year terms, ten-year reigns, fifty-year tyrannies. Those often become our de facto father figures and soon we have no eyes, no need for *THE* Father.

I was teaching in Germany in a Lutheran university during the funeral of Pope John Paul II in 2006 and the election of Benedict XVI. The German Lutherans were watching TV a great deal then, but I have to admit, I wasn't watching much myself. It wasn't too interesting to me, but the Lutherans were really fascinated. Luther would have rolled over in his grave, I suppose. I wondered why they were so interested?

I have done a lot of work with men's spirituality in recent years on what we call the "father wound" and "father hunger." The first time I spoke in Germany was in the late seventies. My book had come out called *Der Wilde Mann*, and I went into the Nuremberg Cathedral to talk about it. It was full to overflowing: they were sitting in the aisles, on the window sills, and on the floor of the sanctuary. I talked to them for almost an hour on the problem of the father. A young man stood up at the end and said: "We want to thank you, Father Richard, for coming here. I want to tell you a little about us German people. In the First World War, we killed all our grandfathers. We were so needy of a father figure, so aimless without a father, that we chose a bad father, and the rest of the world knows what happened to us and to you because of that. Now we live in shame as Germans. Not only did we kill our grandfathers in the First World War, we then killed all our fathers in the Second World War." He choked up and, stretching his arms in both directions, said, "This cathedral is filled with young men; sons without fathers and without grandfathers." I and the crowd were speechless, but no one disagreed or objected to what he said. There were soft tears.

So in 2006, as I watched the papal funeral and the fascination with it, I knew we were not dealing with anything logical as far as the German Lutherans' interest in it. People who were Catholic and didn't agree with most of what John Paul II said were also fascinated by him. This was not reasonable; it is what we call "archetypical." In a world that is so incoherent, so much in flux—where there is no substantial experience of who I am—such a need to latch on to celebrities, to very strong figures, very often to father figures, becomes if not a conscious then certainly an unconscious and compelling need. Add on to this a mantle of holiness, and many move toward the father figure like moths toward a flame. It is a magnet to the soul in need of healing. But without that healing, we will continue to destroy the world by continued wars, ecological devastation, and failed relationships at every level.

In some circles that I've been in, even contemplation and meditation have been ways to seek identity of importance, just like being a charismatic was back in the seventies. I have rarely felt this with Contemplative Outreach or the World Community for Christian Meditation, but do know, Brothers and Sisters, that the disguises of the ego are endless. So we must make sure that, in taking on a spiritual practice, we are not just seeking moral high ground in our own eyes or in the eyes of anybody else. Is meditation leading me to a new vulnerability and intimacy, or the opposite? Is contemplation leading me to what John Main calls *dispossession*, instead of another new possession? Be careful of any *I have* or *I am* language, except the great *I am* that we are in God. Maybe this is one interpretation of Jesus' advice to "pray in secret."

The Yahweh Prayer

And with that notion, let me conclude with something I learned that could change your life. It might be something that you can hold on to much more than more words from me. Every April in Santa Fe, they have this marvelous conference on science, consciousness, and religion. There are about four major scientists speaking each day. By the third speaker, I just had to go back to my room. It might have been the best preached retreat I had ever made. There were no priests or theologians speaking. But scientists spoke, who we once thought were the enemies of religion, but who are becoming our best friends and who now speak of Mystery far better and more honestly than many trained in theology do. Many have a wonderful ability to show there is one world, one truth, with large all-embracing patterns at work in the universe. They have come to this mainly through their own study, which shows the value of dualistic thought, and how it can lead you so—and then beyond! Our advantage as meditators is that we are coming to this same sense of Mystery through our being, which levels the human playing field. We don't have to be smart, we just have to be present.

One of the speakers, a Jewish scientist who was also a rabbi, told us something I had never been told in all my studies of the Hebrew Scriptures. He pointed out something about the word *Yahweh*—the sacred Jewish name for God, which we had been told meant I AM. It was unutterable and literally unspeakable for the Jewish people. During this time they substituted Adonai or Elohim. If you have studied Hebrew, you know that the vowels are not printed, just the consonants, and you fill in the vowels with your eye and mind.

That much I knew, but he took it one step further. He pointed out that even the consonants used in the word *Yahweh* are the Hebrew consonants that do not allow you to close your lips or use your tongue. In fact, the sacred name *Yahweh* is an attempt to imitate and replicate the sound of inhalation and exhalation! Many people were in tears as he went on and made them recognize what the great teachers of meditation have always been teaching us: that God cannot be captured in any form of words that we could control or ideas we could formulate, but was like the very air, breath, spirit in front of our mouth.

The word that archetypal religion came up with for God, for the great I AM, was a word mimicking breath itself! Unspeakable because only breathable: the one thing we have been doing since we came out of our mother's body, and the one thing we will also cease to do when we die and pass into the eternal I AM. Air, breath, wind, and spirit are always beyond us, yet totally around us, within us, and beyond us, and we share in it equally. It is the same air that we all breathe, and yet each of us receives it intimately. No one controls it! It is the utter democratization of religion and offers equal access to the Divine. There is no African or American way to breath. Hindus and Christians breath the same air. I teach this wherever I go, and probably more than anything else, people write back to me that it has changed their entire prayer life and their very capacity for presence to God. Now they pray with conscious loving choice—even while they sleep.

These also are people who have committed them-selves, as John Main says, to "the poverty of a single word," to the poverty of a word that is hardly a word at all. In this case, our very breath. It can't be spoken, it can only be breathed; although now as we understand the autonomic nervous system, *it is really done to us*. We are just the reeds, the instruments, the flutes of God, who allow ourselves to be played.

Silent meditation is the most foundational naming of our mind problem, offering of an answer, and naming of the mystery within us. But there is nothing to possess or claim, usually just a constant experience of our incapacity to pray at all. Eventually we know that *we are being prayed **through***, and all we can do is allow it, like breathing itself. You now know a way to follow Paul's twice-given advice to "pray without ceasing" (1 Thess 5:17; Eph 6:18). It is the best actual church reform that I can imagine, because it comes from the bottom up and the inside out. In the "prayer beyond words," which Jesus clearly teaches here, he instructs the apostles to shut themselves alone in their rooms to pray to the Father "who is in secret" (Matt 6:1–6). Here, we move beyond any attachment to, infatuation with, or defense of any single form and go back to the poverty of a single word and the simplicity of our every breath.

Chapter Four

RELIGION:
A TRANSFORMATIONAL SYSTEM?

To continue our metaphor of the lever and a place to stand, I think that, when you end up standing where mass culture or cultural Christianity is standing, you have almost no leverage to really change the world. We have little to offer from an alternative spiritual perspective, and I'm afraid in many ways that is what has happened to Western religion. We have more "civil religion" than any new mind and heart of Christ (e.g., Eph 4:23–24). I think it is important that we understand how we got into this position of religion as a belonging system or a mere belief system, and not actually the radical transformational system that Jesus seemed to be desiring.

Let me give you a helpful paradigm for understanding our problem. E. F. Schumacher, who wrote *Small is Beautiful*, also wrote *Guide for the Perplexed*. Remember, Neil Postman said it's precisely perplexity that we avoid. Schumacher leads us right into seeming perplexity, but then out the other side too. His explanation, which I very much agree with, is that he sees the three parts of the Hebrew Scriptures—Law, Prophets, and Wisdom—as representing the three stages of developing consciousness. He says we have to begin our spiritual journey precisely where Jewish revelation begins, and that is with Torah: Law, structure,

29

identity, boundaries, certitude, order, authority, and clarity. That is how we can best form a healthy, happy, and secure ego structure. I sure agree with that.

The alternative is the disaster that we have in the post-modern world where it is all a big open field, with the immature ego free to pick and choose without any preparation or foundation in any tradition. You are forced to be the center of the world because there is no other center except your freedom to choose, prefer, and decide—moment by moment. This does not help you grow up at all, and when you do become adult in age, you tend to feel very entitled—and very poorly prepared for community, friendship, marriage, job, humility, patience, or any kind of union, much less the great divine union. In short, it gives you tasks you are unprepared for, and inflates your ego far beyond what it deserves. You and I are not the center of anything, except perhaps our mother's early attention. It creates a lethal combination of ignorance and arrogance at the same time, which some say is the very name of the modern and post-modern self.

So if you stay with the first task of life too long, creating and maintaining your own ego structure, you tend to have a good "container," but you never get beyond the container to the "contents" of life itself. *You have learned to rely almost exclusively upon outer authorities that have now become inner conditioning.* There must be something more than "Law," or you have no need to go on any journey at all, much less a journey of faith. Outer authority tells me what the truth is, tells me what to do, tells me what is right and wrong. It's a good place to start; in many ways, it is a necessary place to start. It's the parent/child relationship that later takes the form of master/pupil and then, if we are lucky, teacher/disciple. We have to have other people to tell us that this is good, or everybody has to start again at zero.

Healthy cultures always had elders and traditions so we did not have to do that all by ourselves, as if we could anyway. This early need is exactly what we see in books like some parts of Exodus, and surely Leviticus and Numbers. There it appears in the form of laws, strong boundary keeping, much impulse control, clear group symbols, and the necessity of strict conformity with all of these. This is how religion must almost always start. It keeps you inside the right boxing ring until you know what the real issues are, and what is worth fighting for.

Most religions stay at this level of Leviticus and Numbers religion. It is a good belonging system with clear boundaries and identity. It takes away most self-doubt, and thus people are often quite happy at this stage, if they can succeed at it. It is largely patriarchal, authoritative, top-down religion. After a while one gets so invested in doing the task of Law, and maintaining social and personal order, that we almost always think that *that* is what religion is for! Paul devoted two of his letters, Romans and Galatians, almost entirely to this problem, and yet we continue to do the same today, as if he did not write them. Why? I don't think it is ill will on anybody's part. I personally think it is a lack of contemplative seeing. If people do not go deeper into the mystery of things, religion as container is quite sufficient for most of them. It takes away their anxiety, it holds them together, it provides a level of happiness, and so it must be the godly thing. Belonging to groups, feeling the emotion around loyalty symbols, saying "I believe" in this or that, is what the older Catholic tradition once called the first third of the spiritual journey, the "purgative way." It purges us from our basic narcissism and allows us to commit and learn a bit of self-sacrifice, but it is nowhere close to the second and third stages, the illuminative, or the truly unitive, paths toward God.

When I look at the American Christian Churches since 9/11, it seems that church has frequently become one more place for frightened people to hide. It often became a way to give ourselves a quick fix of surety and of "God is on our side," so that we would not have to look at this issue with any subtlety or repentance whatsoever. What if the president had called a worldwide convocation of Islamic peoples to ask them: "Why do you hate us so much? What are we doing wrong? What could we do better to show you that we are your friends?" Unthinkable, isn't it? It was even unthinkable to people who go to church each Sunday. Why? I believe it is because most organized religion is still a "first half of life" religion. (See "A Spirituality for the Two Halves of Life," a recorded conference by Richard Rohr and Paula D'Arcy, available through the Center for Action and Contemplation in Albuquerque, New Mexico, at www. cacradicalgrace.org). We are usually and forever shoring up the container and seldom getting to the unitive or even illuminative contents of it all.

There is a second section of the Hebrew Scriptures that we call "Prophets." Without doubt this part has been the most ignored, the least quoted, and the least influential for Christians, and I am told for Jews, too. I suspect that, because prophets are always presenting an alternative prospective, they are loyal critics, which is a hard position to hold. He or she is an insider, but *on the edge of the inside*. It is not just a rare position to hold, but also to pass on and to legitimate, yet Paul lists it as the second most important role for the building up of the church (1 Cor 12:28). Wow, what ever happened to that?

Well, no group likes internal critics: they look disloyal and dangerous. No surprise that, according to Jesus, the prophets were all killed (Matt 23:29–36). It was precisely their mystical encounter that gives them their authority, and not any ordination or official validation. It is pretty amazing that their books were included in the canonical texts, since they so deeply criticized the secular and religious establishments. It is forever to the credit of the Jewish people that they institutionalized this pattern of self-criticism in Scripture. You know how rare that is, and it surely has not been the pattern of Christianity, which has normally excluded most inner critics as heretics, rebels, or unbelievers.

Once we move to the prophetic level, there is an emergence of inner authority. First you had almost exclusive reliance upon outer authority. Then—once you begin to know for yourself, once you've gone deep and have met the Holy One at some level—you find that your reliance upon outer authority lessens. You become rather dangerous at that stage because what most people do is dualistically switch their allegiance totally to their own inner authority. We see it in most teenagers. This is probably the rebellion of the sixties and the continuing chaos since that time: we call it postmodernism. Many people are so angry and disillusioned with where outer authority has led history and governments and churches that they pull all authority inside themselves: "I won't trust any tradition, any big explanation, anything except my experiences. I will personally create any needed meanings," they seem to say.

Schumacher wisely says that what maturity does and what the Hebrew Scriptures do is lead us to a third stage symbolized by biblical Wisdom Literature, which invariably struggles with paradox and mystery—and leaves us there—while also creating a new but deeper synthesis. This would be especially true in the Book of Job, many of the psalms, the Book of Ecclesiastes, some of proverbs, and some of the Book of Sirach. These books are not conventional wisdom but alternative wisdom, or, in our language, contemplative and nondualistic wisdom. It probably reaches both its summit and a kind of dead end in the Book of Job, where the psyche is finally mature enough to have faith in the form of darkness instead of light, whereas stage 1 insists upon total light and explanation, as we see in fundamentalism today.

The Book of Job is just waiting and preparing for someone like Jesus. Jesus represents the mature religious position where finally we have a person doing, as it were, a faith-filled dance between inner and outer authority, *and achieving a new Unified Field that can include both light and darkness*. That is Schumacher's "guide for the perplexed." He says this third task of living with paradox cannot be tackled until one has walked the first two. It is a sequential journey. If you stay just in stage 1 conformity or stage 2 criticism, you are in no way ready for mystery, paradox, the collision of opposites that is the cross, or, quite simply, adult faith. You are really not capable of anything except dualist either/or thinking. That is the best explanation I have found for why most religion remains so immature.

Further, Schumacher makes it very clear that the movement from stage 1 to stage 2 is experienced as a major dying. If you are not trained in dying, you won't go! Most people are not trained in dying, in that *dispossession* that John Main talks about. To fall back into the Source will first feel more like losing than growing, more like dying than achieving, especially if we have been building and maintaining our personal container for forty years. As I learned when I wrote *Adam's Return*, my book on male initiation rites, at the heart of every mature religion is the same message: "You must die before you die" (Crossroad, 2004). There is no exception to that in any world religion, yet we prefer to talk only about being born again, forgetting that something cannot be born again unless the something first dies. The idea is really very dishonest and will not work spiritually.

Any religion that tells you differently—that it can all be a learning curve of upward success—is lying to you. That is not how transformation happens. That's why we don't have transformative religion but largely religion as a belonging system; religion as a belief system that really asks almost nothing of you; or religion as a reward/punishment system, which, of course, doesn't really invite you to fall in love with God at all, but relies upon conformity, along with disguised threat, shame, and fear.

Francis McNutt, the former Dominican who popularized the ministry of healing back in the 1970s, wrote a book called *The Nearly Perfect Crime.* In his decades' long study of healing in the church, he noted, among many things, that we largely lost the very word *healing* in the mainline Christian churches. It was not even part of our vocabulary until he wrote his first book *Healing,* back in the 1970s. The sacrament was called "extreme unction" and, as the name reveals, was put off till the last hours of life. Why not, if the only real goal is the next world? When McNutt first popularized the notion of healing prayer and healing services, Catholics all thought, "Well, this must come from the Protestants; we are not into healing!" And of course, they were right! Most Catholics didn't expect to really heal people, inner or outer, and as priests, we felt our job was to absolve sin, rather than actually transform people. "Get rid of the contaminating element," as it were, rather than, "Learn what you can about yourself and God because of this conflict." Those are two very different paths. So maybe it *is* the "nearly perfect crime" in light of the fact that in the four Gospels Jesus did two things over and over again: *he preached and he healed.* We do a lot of preaching, but not too much healing. We did not know how.

I am now strongly convinced that if our preaching does not effect in the listener some level of healing, then it's not even the Gospel. Healing is the most simple criterion of preaching the Word that I could imagine. The truth heals and expands one in its very hearing, and "the truth will make you free" (John 8:32). It allows and presses you to reconfigure the world with plenty of room for gentleness and peace for yourself and for those around you. *The lived Gospel then moves more by inherent attraction than direct promotion.* As a preacher of forty years, I know that all we do is get the ball rolling, but it is not itself the ball.

If there isn't much linkage between our religion and our politics, I think it's because we are not into the healing of ourselves. So how can we understand the healing of the world? Only whole people can imagine or call forth a more whole world. To be into healing depends on relating with love and compassion. Do not hear me unkindly, but official religion is usually into imputing and then forgiving guilt. This is much more sin management than proclaiming a larger than life vision for humanity. Remember what we said earlier: *The ego contracts around problems. The soul gathers and is drawn by meaning.* We clergy settle for the lesser but more commonly expected agenda. It really is the best way to keep the laity coming back, strangely enough. I wish it did not work so well.

If we let you know any form of contemplation or meditation, where you would know the mercy of God for yourself, you would not be so codependent upon us as clergy. Although it is not done maliciously, this is called job security. We all have a hard time doing things that essentially work ourselves out of a job, or make ourselves unnecessary. Sin management does hold the flock together, but soon one realizes there is little maturity or even love in a flock that is so well held together. I have been a priest for forty years now, and the amazingly passive, passive-dependent, and passive-aggressive nature of much of the church is rather obvious to many of us. That is what happens when you do not teach people how to pray, which is to move from Law to Prophets to Wisdom almost naturally and on its own kind of schedule: outer authority to inner authority to what Merton well calls "the General Dance."

Growing Up Spiritually

Up to now, much of human history has been in the first stage of consciousness. It is nobody's fault. We lived at survival levels and needed to circle the wagons around our own group, national identity, or ethnicity. We needed absolute beliefs even if they were not always true. So when the floodgates opened on a broad level in the 1960s, many of us tasted the first heady fruits of critical thinking. It was intoxicating, half true, and dangerous. The immediate results were often impressive. The hippies were my own generation, and we thought that the final stage of enlightenment was achieved in prophetic criticism of the Vietnam war, the legalistic and clerical church, and the racist, classist society. It was surely needed, I am now more convinced than ever. People who never lived through it, or fought for it, can nostalgically dream about how wonderful things were before the deluge. If only they knew how neurotic, prejudiced, smug, and small so much of 1950s America and Catholicism really was. The only ones who can idealize it are those who were either not alive then, as we see in some of our young priests, or not aware of what was happening. Ask people of color, gays and lesbians, battered wives faithful to their marriages, and the untold victims of incest and pedophilia that no one talked about.

However, everyone gets tired of critique after a while. You cannot build on exclusively negative or critical energy. You can only build on life and what you are *for*, not what you are against. It keeps you in a state of victimhood and/or a state of anger, and, frankly, it's immature if you stall there for long. It is a bit like blaming one's parents for everything. Mere critique and analysis are not salvation; they are not liberation. Mere critique and analysis are not spacious. They are not wonderful at all. No one or no group likes to be critiqued every day and told they are wrong or stupid. It becomes another form of stage 2 righteousness on the Left instead of stage 1 righteousness on the Right, and, like any form of self-righteousness, it's something that everyone needs to move beyond. They are just two different forms of ego.

We only become enlightened as the ego dies to its pretenses, and we begin to be led by soul and Spirit. That dying is something we are led through by the grace of God and by confronting our own shadow. As we learn to move into a Larger Realm, we will almost naturally weep over those sins, as we recognize that we are everything that we hate and attack in other people. Then we begin to live the great mystery of compassion that we will call stage 3.

Jesus as a Wisdom (Stage 3) Person

The reason Christianity became a separate religion was because Jesus so beautifully symbolized a further stage in human possibility and consciousness. We finally had a man who could clearly deal with opposites and contradictions and people outside of his own little world. He never taught a reward/punishment system; he never taught a religion. His worldview was much closer to a win/win scenario than the later win/lose game we made it into. You know, if we are honest about our seeming criteria, *just about everybody loses and deserves punishment more than reward.*

Psychologist Lawrence Kohlberg, in his study of the levels of moral development, showed ethical maturity through six levels. He said that we can normally understand people just one level above ourselves. So, if you are a person of level-3 moral development, with a little stretch, you perhaps can be sympathetic to level-4 people—on a good day! Well Jesus was a level-6 person. If most of religion is happily ensconced at levels 2 and 3, as it seems to be, Jesus and his teaching goes right over most of our heads. "Love those who hate you and persecute you!" We basically don't get it and do not agree with it. He does not compute with our software. Most of Jesus' teaching on nonviolence, simplicity, downward mobility, forgiveness of enemies, and inclusivity, has had no strong effect on the entire history of Christianity, except on those few in every generation and every denomination who do the full journey—inner and outer. We must start being honest about this.

So that we can be a little more sympathetic to our history of blatant unfaithfulness to our own Jesus, let us set this in context with a little scriptural and historical development of why we stalled largely inside stage 1's "Law and Order." Apart from almost nonstop war, barbarian invasions, the Black Plague, famine, and oppression in most Christian countries for the first 1500 years, most of the nails were in the coffin of stage 1 already by the year 313, when Constantine made Christianity the established religion of the

Roman Empire. To hold an empire together, you need conformity, you need wars, you need authority—and you need enemies. Religion was not needed in the West for enlightenment and transformation of persons, but to create good citizens for emperor and pope. We were not wanted or allowed as an alternative; we had become the establishment, perhaps noticing the poor from our Episcopal palaces, which one still sees all over Europe. Overnight we literally moved from catacombs to basilicas. We still call our great Catholic churches "basilicas"—which literally means "palaces," and this is indeed the setting in which we worshipped.

Once Pharaoh was your benefactor and protector, there were a lot of questions you couldn't ask anymore. You could not ask about liberation of slaves while in Pharaoh's house. Nor did questions of justice or equality make it to the dining room table. And if someone did ask such questions, he would not be answered but quietly—or savagely—eliminated. That already became clear in Exodus, or it was supposed to anyway. Once we were the top, we could no longer feel the rejection that Jesus structurally put himself into by being born poor in an occupied country. We had changed sides, and therefore we had changed our point of viewing. We saw, not from the bottom up, as Jesus did, but from the top down. The top was where almost all the clergy henceforth resided. That is the perspective that almost all our preaching and Scripture interpretation came from: white, European, educated, comfortable, usually celibate males. I am one myself, and we are not all bad. But we are not *all*.

Let's go back to the very concept of God's justice, which begins to be revealed in Torah. You see, if you are God, you don't have any criteria outside yourself that you can conform to and make yourself just. The way God is, is simply God's faithfulness to who God is. God can only be true to God's own criteria. So for God to be just, therefore, is for him to be faithful to what he has said and who he is. This is very different from any vengeful retaliatory understanding of justice, which is the later juridical understanding. What we are going to see after 313 is that the church criminalized the notion of sin. The church took on the juridical function of the state. However, what God does and what God reveals in the Scriptures is that *God uses Israel's sin, God uses our mistakes, **to bring us to transformation**. Such "restorative justice" is the real and final meaning of biblical justice.* God is always using people's mistakes in their favor to transform them. This is our stage 3 Wisdom Jesus!

The Bible as a Text Struggling Forward

You can't find an exception to that in all the great biblical heroes, except Jesus and Mary themselves. Their weaknesses become the means of God's grace. Our capacity for missing the point, however, is understandable because the ego/flesh naturally reads reality as tit for tat, quid pro quo, and reward and punishment. If you do it wrong, you deserve punishment; if you do it right, life rewards you: it's the same story line as in every bad novel. And that's what we have made the Bible into—a bad novel based on the only story line we are really interested in, where the good guys win and the bad guys lose. It makes sense unless, of course, you are losing, suffering, sinning, or hating yourself. Then you hope for something different. It is to that hope that Jesus came and to that hope that he most profoundly spoke.

The Bible—which, for Christians, reached its omega point in Jesus—is an alternative reading of history, a "text in travail," as René Girard puts it; a text that partly gets it, but then it seems too good to be true, and it backtracks. The text itself illustrates all three stages. It gets the message and holds it now and then, but invariably decides it cannot possibly believe that the Good News could be that good, or that God could be that generous, and then it begins to put conditions, prerequisites, and requirements and reverts back to stage 1. As I say in my book *Things Hidden* (St. Anthony Messenger, 2008), the entire Bible is always three steps forward, two steps backward; the answer is included in the problem.

God's one-of-a-kind job description is that God actually uses our problems to lead us to the full answer. God is the perfect Recycler, and in the economy of grace, nothing is wasted. God does not destroy the devil, but uses the devil for his own purposes, which is the ultimate victory, it seems to me.

So God's power for justice is precisely God's power to restore the people when they are broken or hurt and to use their mistakes to liberate them, to soften them, to enlighten them, and to transform them. There is no text in the Old Testament where God's justice is equated with vengeance on the sinner. It might look like it, but if you read the whole paragraph and look at the context, chastisement is always meant to bring us back. God's justice is always saving justice. What is experienced as punishment is always for the sake of restoration, not for vengeance. Therefore, the justice of the people is to participate in this wholeness and spaciousness of God, to be brought into God's same non-vengeful freedom. If we have not gotten to first base with nonviolence in Christian countries, is it perhaps because we never nipped it in the bud within ourselves? That is first of all the work of prayer. You must face all your demons interiorly in inner journeys, in shadowboxing your own illusions, in naming, forgiving, and healing your own darkness and brokenness, or you will never know how to do it outside. Take that as a given.

I already used the Book of Leviticus to illustrate stage 1 religion, but just so we don't dualistically understand any book of the Bible as either totally perfect or utterly out- dated, let's note that there is a capsulized statement of stage 3 wisdom already in Leviticus, which most of us have back- tracked from now! In fact, Americans would probably call it socialism or even communism. The text says: "The land shall not be sold in perpetuity, for the land is mine; with me you are but aliens and tenants....If any of your kin fall into diffi- culty and become dependent on you, you shall support them; they shall live with you as though resident aliens. Do not take interest in advance or otherwise make a profit from them, but fear your God; let them live with you" (Lev 25:23, 35–36). This rather enlightened text on the sin of usury lasted until the twelfth century in the Western Church and flies in the face of capitalism that we now take as a given. Until then, to take interest on a loan when someone was down and out meant excommunication from the church.

Now, there are people who say that the church never changes. It is funny, in some areas we can change very eas- ily; I wish there were space here to list them. When it comes to capitalistic thinking, we can drop Scripture and Tradition in a moment. What was once a "mortal sin" is now the very name of our Western Christian economies. *Capitalism* is the making of money from money itself, or "capital," rather than from actual labor, producing goods and services. It solidifies its point by grounding it in the very nature of God: *"I am the* LORD *your God, who brought you out of the land of Egypt, to give you the land of Canaan"* (Lev 25:38). In other words, "You got your land free from me, Israel. I own it, so you better give it away freely!" All hinges on that initial God-experience. Now, if you haven't had that initial God experience, you won't understand that and won't know how to pass on what you haven't experienced. Everything depends upon knowing the Holy One, and once you know the Holy One, the Mystery will flow through you. The trinitarian dance will begin. So you see what I am trying to say: there were ancient Jews in stage 3, while, as we will see in a moment, many contemporary Christians are happily ensconced in stage 1. It all depends on those who "know the Lord, and his ways," or, in our language, those who have an inner life of ego-decreasing, shadow-exposing, glory-revealing prayer. We call it meditation or contemplation, because the word *prayer* no longer connotes that inner journey anymore for most people. In our practical and utilitarian cultures, prayer became another way to "get" something, when it is really much more about "letting go" of something, all the things that we do not need and that are not real anyway.

To sum up: If our "guide to the perplexed" is that spiritual consciousness moves from Law to Prophecy to Wisdom, I have tried to show that Jesus himself is the Living Word who can be shown to *affirm* all three stages. But without doubt, he finally and fully *represents* the maturity of stage 3 Wisdom. Such wholeness almost inevitably would call forth a whole new religion. Yet, as I tried to illustrate in several ways, and especially in the last example from Leviticus, there are succinct and wonderful examples of stage 3 Wisdom throughout the Bible, so we dare not dualistically and cleanly divide the "Old" from the "New" Testaments. Jesus is simply Judaism at its best, and comes fully from that divine matrix. Finally, I believe that an inner life of meditation or contemplation is made to order to grease the wheels that move us along the path to Wisdom. Without it, we will always stall at mere Law or mere criticism.

Chapter Five

PASSING THROUGH THE EYE
OF THE NEEDLE

The key to entering into the Divine Exchange is never our worthiness but always God's graciousness. Any attempt to measure or increase our worthiness will always fall short, or it will force us into the position of denial and pretend, which produces the constant perception of hypocrisy in religious people.

To switch to an "economy of grace" is a switch that's very hard for humans to make. We base almost everything in human culture on achievement, performance, accomplishment, payment, exchange value, or worthiness of some sort. I call it meritocracy. *Unless one personally experiences a dramatic and personal breaking of the rules of merit, it is almost impossible to disbelieve or operate outside of its rigid logic. This cannot happen theoretically or abstractly. It cannot happen "out there"!*

Our word for that dramatic breaking of the ironclad rule is *grace*. It is God's magnificent release from our self-made prisons, and the only way that God's economy can triumph over our strongly internalized merit-badge system. Grace is the secret key whereby God offers to be the Divine Locksmith for every life and for all of history. Life, when lived fully, tends to tool and retool us until we eventually find this key is necessary for our very survival and sanity.

Without grace, almost everything human declines and devolves into smallness, hurt, and blame.

Grace humiliates our attempts at private virtue. Grace makes us feel powerless, where before, we knew that if we did *this*, then we would earn *that*. Accepting grace can make us feel poor and empty and even useless. Who wants grace? Only sinners! Almost no one else. Only prostitutes, drunkards and tax collectors, not the proper people. Not the nice or successful people, who have no need for any gaps to be filled. They have filled them all themselves.

Perhaps that's why Jesus taught that most outrageous thing that I'm still scandalized by: "It is easier for a camel to go through the eye of a needle than for someone who is rich to enter the kingdom of God" (Mark 10:25). Now, why didn't we make that rather clear teaching into one of our dogmas or moral mandates? People can't go to communion if they are a practicing homosexual or are in a second marriage without the first being annulled, but they can go to communion all they want if they are multimillionaires—in a world of poor people. One begins to see that we have all and always been "cafeteria Christians," picking and choosing what we were ready to hear. If you look closely, you will see that *the things we emphasize as truly sinful are almost always body-based, and the things we pick as absolutely essential are those that tie us to dependence upon the clergy*. I am not being unfair. Check it out for yourself, and then notice how different this selective morality is from the radical morality of Jesus.

Jesus tells his followers: "Set your heart on God's kingdom and God's justice first, and all these other things will be taken care of" (Matt 6:33, my translation). Any of you who are involved in church work know that the kiss of death to any lecture series or parish program is to put the word *justice* in the title. You can be assured of a very small attendance, and the program will often have to be canceled for lack of interest. Now, how did we get to such a place that the things Jesus clearly deemed unimportant—and things he never once talked about (e.g., birth control, abortion, and homosexuality)—have become the very litmus tests of Christian faith? And largely in the last twenty-five years, by people who dare to call themselves traditional or conservative? The fundamentals of the faith were quite different in the church's first 1900 years; in fact, they were settled in the early centuries and were called the Apostles' Creed and the Nicene Creed. I do not think these have changed, and I also note their lack of moralism. They are much more mystical and cosmological. They inserted you into a Big Picture, a meta-narrative where you belonged and were saved, not by your moral perfection or performance, but by God's gracious mercy, inclusion, and initiative.

Now, I do not want to say that Jesus does not recommend some strong moral decisions, but they mostly have to do with changing ourselves and not always trying to change other people. Let me give you one hard one-liner that hardly any of us have not been troubled by, starting with the initial astonishment of the disciples: "None of you can become my disciple if you do not give up all your possessions" (Luke 14:33). This rather clear passage has not been followed to my knowledge by the papacy, the episcopacy, the priesthood, or the laity. In fact, Christian countries tend to lead the way in the pursuit of luxury and in massive consumption of the goods of this earth.

The only reason I'm daring to say this is because Jesus said it. (I haven't lived this myself either, and I'm supposed to be a Franciscan besides being a Christian.) The man who is often called the "thirteenth would-be apostle," the only one who turned away from a personal invitation by Jesus, is also given a clear prerequisite for following him: "*There is still one thing lacking,*" he tells the rich young man. "*Sell all that you own and distribute the money to the poor, and you will have treasure in heaven; then come, follow me*" (Luke 18:22). It is astounding really that Jesus would dare to say this and to name conversion in such a practical and demanding way, yet perhaps one reason his answer is so hard is because it is an egocentric question from a man who is both young and rich. The man had provoked this answer by asking: "Good Teacher, what must I do to inherit eternal life?" (v. 18). The question shows no high degree of enlightenment or love; it is just glorified and delayed self-interest. Yet we have let people ask that question for centuries and even let them think it is the right question. It's disguised narcissism, religion as an insurance policy, not love of God at all. Note that Jesus actually refuses to answer the question directly, because it is a well-disguised selfish question. He just tells the rich boy, in effect, "It is going to take major surgery for you to grow up. Without some clear downward mobility, you will never get it." Passages like this, which ask us to change ourselves, are normally treated today as pious nonsense.

Jesus knows that he cannot give this young man another ego possession and let him call it heaven or salvation; the young man has been collecting too long and it is time for him to pay back. "He became sad, for he was very rich," the story says. Jesus then looked around and said to his disciples, "How hard it is for those who have wealth to enter the kingdom of God!" (Luke 18:23–24). In another place he tells his disciples explicitly: "You cannot serve God and wealth" (16:13). Then the text says, "The Pharisees, who were lovers of money, heard all this, and they ridiculed him"—perhaps just as we would. But Jesus then goes even further and immediately adds: "*You are those who justify*

yourselves in the sight of others; but God knows your hearts; for
what is prized by human beings is an abomination in the eyes
of God" (16:14–15). Here we see Jesus as an astute psychologist, who recognizes and exposes things that we only
now have names for: the seeking of status, false motives, creation of a persona, cultivation of a self-image, and denial.

Yet, kind Jesus does give us all some wiggle room.
Toward the beginning of his Sermon on the Mount, he says,
"Unless your righteousness *exceeds that of the scribes and*
Pharisees, you will never enter the kingdom of heaven" (Matt
5:20). Now listen to that closely. He is not denying that
there is a level of virtue or righteousness at stage 1 religion.
Who wouldn't like a loyal soldier, who is on time, clean, and
reverent; who salutes you, and does not steal from you?
(See "Discharging Your Loyal Soldier," a recorded Web cast,
available at www.cacradicalgrace.org.) Who wouldn't like it
if all the world showed a sense of basic social order and concern? And yet Jesus, in effect, says, "But that's not what I'm
here to talk about. I am not here so polite society can continue to be polite." But that first stage need is what we have
largely made of Jesus' message. Loyal West Point cadets are
great for empire building, and on many levels to be
admired, but just don't call that job description the same as
the job description for a disciple of Jesus. We have done
that, I am afraid, in Catholic schools, religious life, seminaries, and the priesthood. Loyal soldiers will always get can-
onized; mystics and prophets maybe, but even then we will
wait a few centuries till we can make sure we can refashion
them into loyal soldiers of the institution. I wonder how
you would do that with John the Baptist? Or Francis and
Clare of Assisi? Their very lifestyles shouted out reform, as
well as very critical thinking about mainline religion.

The disciple is one who hears what Jesus said: "Do not worry about your life, what you will eat, or about your body, what you will wear....It is the nations of the world that strive after all these things....Instead, strive for [the Father's] kingdom" (Luke 12:22, 30–31). To my knowledge, there is no taboo against five-star restaurants, cosmetic surgery, or designer clothing. You would think there might be from above statements. Jesus, by the way, only talks about clothing three times and in each case he dismisses its importance or even mocks it. In the above passage he says it is the pagans "who worry about what they are to wear"; another time he makes fun of the clergy "who like to walk around in long robes" (Mark 12:38); and finally, in his tirade against those who sit on Moses' chair (vv. 13), he points out that they have made the fringes on their clothing long so that others will see them (v. 5). You would think we clergy would go out of our way never to wear any long robe whatsoever, and certainly not hang tassels at the end of our stoles, which of course is exactly what we do. I do it myself.

The women of the world, who have sometimes been told they are too concerned with dress, jewelry, and design, must shudder if they attend any high-church Catholic function. We clergy outdo you any day! I love my brown Franciscan habit, but I hope I know I am a Franciscan even when I am not wearing it, and can exchange it if it is going to create a barrier for anyone or from anyone.

You can usually correlate any *preoccupation* with externals with a lack of deep inner experience of the Mystery. Once you have touched upon the Absolute, all externals become mere containers, costumes, and signposts, but not even close to the contents. What has to die is not just our self-image, which is to some degree necessary, but, much more important, *our attachment to our self-image*; for myself, for example, any need to protect or project that I am a priest, or bishop, or cardinal or even head of the local prayer group. That means nothing to the True Self. It is mere window dressing, but when our windows have too much self-conscious dressing hanging on them, you often never see beyond the window itself. Much of "high church" is still back in the days of the Book of Leviticus, written by the priests in love with "smells and bells," and too preoccupied with the sanctuary instead of the world and the people God is suffering with.

Jesus, perhaps disappointingly, gives no abstract theory of social justice. Instead, just like St. Francis will do, he makes his life *a concrete living parable of how to live in this world*. He demands of his first followers a living witness to a simple life *on the edge*, because once you are at the visible center, once you are on the top, you have too much to prove and too much to protect; every great spiritual teacher has warned against it. The only free positions in this world are at the bottom and at the edges of things. Everywhere else, you have too much to maintain—an image to promote and a fear of losing it all—which ends up controlling your whole life. I do not think that is much of an exaggeration, and Jesus says the same in more than one place. Now and then, read Luke 12:22–34 on not worrying about our life as a meditation, and let's all ask ourselves if that is really our worldview. It was my father Francis's favorite!

A Bit of History

Much of what Jesus said seems to have been understood rather clearly in that first several-hundred-year period, almost taken for granted before the imperial edict of 313 that pushed us to the top and the center of the Roman

Empire; things like nonparticipation in war, simplicity of lifestyle, and love of enemies, which have not been part of mainstream Christianity for many centuries now. But let's look at the very early period for a bit.

The *Didache* (see *The Teaching of the Twelve: Believing & Practicing the Primitive Christianity of the Didache Community*, by Tony Jones, Paraclete Press, 2009) was written around AD 90 and is a paramount illustration of all that I am talking about here. Among many other wise things, it says: "Share all things with your brother [*sic*]; and do not say that they are your own. If you are sharers in what is imperishable, how much more in things which perish." In books like the *Didache*, you can still touch upon pure and simple Christianity, still untouched by empire, rationalization, and compromise, yet very tender and loving too.

The *Shepherd of Hermas*, written around AD 120, gives us the image of the church as a tower built of white round stones that are not suitable for use in construction. They are not rejected, but they are put away to one side. He said these stones represent those believers who are still relying upon their wealth and success and therefore cannot really build this new community. They cannot really be used until they have been reshaped and something has been taken from them. That something, he says, is their wealth.

St. Clement of Alexandria wrote a letter around the year 175 entitled "Can a Rich Man be Saved?" (See *Opera Omnia* in *Greek Fathers*, Migne.) The very fact that it was still an active question gives us the early picture of how much Jesus was still taken seriously. St. Clement, in fact, concludes that it is not necessary to renounce *all* your worldly possessions to be a believer, but it is surely questionable to be rich.

Tertullian, another father of the church, around the year 200 writes: "If anyone is worried by his family possessions, we advise him, as do many biblical texts, to scorn worldly things. There can be no better exhortation to the abandonment of wealth than the example of our Jesus who had no material possessions. He always defended the poor and He always condemned the rich" (see Tertullian, *The Apology* in *The Ante-Nicene Fathers*, Hendrickson Publishing, 1995).

How did we lose that free position? The church at this point is a nonimperial church, and is still countercultural. After that AD 313 change of structural position, Christianity will increasingly accept and even defend the dominant social order, especially in regard to war and money. Morality becomes individualized into largely sexual morality. It slowly loses its free and alternative vantage point, which is probably why what we now call "religious life" began and flourished after 313. People went to the edges of the church and took vows of poverty, living in satellites that became "little churches," without ever formally leaving the big Church. But it has always been a delicate balancing act, as you see in the lives of almost all founders and foundresses.

I've taken the vow of poverty, for example, but I'm probably more secure today than many of you, because the Franciscans are going to take care of me till I die, and bail me out if I get in trouble. Well, what did the founders historically mean by that poorly named "vow of poverty"? It was a structural statement about standing outside of the whole world of the market, of production and consumption, of quid pro quo thinking. It was a choice for structural insecurity. Once the climbing "market mind" overtakes the soul, it pretty well destroys any possibility of understanding grace and transformation and the active power of God. I remember when my novice master told us, almost whispering, "You know we Franciscans are really communists! But don't tell anybody because that is bad in America."

If you look at texts in the hundred years period preceding 313, it is unthinkable that a Christian would fight in the army. The army is killing Christians; *we* are on the bottom. By the year 400, the entire army has become Christian, and we are now killing the pagans. In a two-hundred-year period, we go from being almost complete outsiders to pretty much directing the inside! Once you are inside, you have to defend your power.

It is in this period that people like St. John Cassian, Evagrius Ponticus, and the early monks go off to Egypt, Syria, and the desert, because they are the first group who says this lifestyle is unacceptable. It is in the desert, we believe, that formal teaching on the different mind that is contemplation first became systematized and taught. Since this point until the modern period, it was assumed and protected by emperors that monks and Christian priests could not fight in war or kill. Why this split between two brands of Christianity? Laity could kill, while we could not and should not—even as recently as when I was up for enlistment in the Vietnam War. I got an immediate deferment because I was a Franciscan. I wonder even more, was there a connection between our deeper hearing of the Gospel through the contemplative mind that did not allow us to kill other people? I surely hope so.

Let me sum up this attempt at an alternative perspective on the Gospels, and the alternative mind that is offered in meditation, by a short example from what we call grief work. I have found that almost like nothing else, people are often deeply transformed during and after major grief, if they allow it to teach them, of course, because our usual defenses do not work when we are grieving.

In our men's rites of passage (see the description at www.malespirituality.org), we send the men out for an intense "grief day," which has always been an essential part of most initiation rites, and I finally know why. The grieving mode, you see, is an entirely different mode of knowing than the fixing mode, the controlling mode, or even the understanding mode. In grief work, you know you do not understand, and you never will. One is plunged into unsolvable absurdity and mystery, often with no end in sight. I now see it as the privileged portal for many people, men in particular, into the world of soul and spirit, because it is the first kind of pain or experience that they cannot fix, change, control, understand, or blame anybody for. Not that we won't try! I am here equating grief work with any forced acts of solidarity with the human tragedy, with the pain on this earth and the injustice and absurdity of it all, usually involving death of someone very close to us.

Through this kind of *closeness to suffering*, we are pulled out of our heads and into our hearts and sobs; we are finally thrown into the belly of the whale, where all transformation and enlightenment happens, in my experience; so much so that Jesus said that "no sign will be given...except the sign of the prophet Jonah" (Matt 13:39). Rather amazing, really. Yet not at all, because only exposure to the downside, the shadow self—the "tragic sense of life," as Miguel de Unamuno called it—tends to change people at any depth. I am now convinced that is true.

Any overly protected life does not know deeply or broadly. So Jesus did not call us to the poor and to the pain just to be helpful to them, although that is wonderful, too. He called us there for *fundamental solidarity with the **real*** and, from that, to the *transformation of ourselves*. We do not go to the edge just to help others, but only later do we realize that it was really to let them help us, in ways we never knew we needed. It is called by some of us "reverse mission." *The ones we think we are saving end up saving us and, in the process, redefine the very meaning of salvation.*

Only near the poor, close to "the tears of things," outside of climbing, and in solidarity with suffering, can we understand ourselves, love one another well, imitate Jesus, and live his full Gospel. The view *from the top of anything* is too filled with misperception, illusions, fear of falling, and a radical disconnection from the heart. You cannot risk climbing there or staying there too long. As Thomas Merton said, you spend your whole life climbing the ladder of success, and when you get to the top you realize it is leaning against the wrong wall.

I have believed for years that in the end there are really only two "cauldrons of transformation": great love and great suffering. And they are indeed cauldrons, big stew pots of warming, boiling, mixing, and flavoring! Our lives of contemplation are a *gradual, chosen, and eventual free fall* into both of these cauldrons. There is no softer or more honest way to say it. Love and suffering are indeed the paths, and contemplative journeys of prayer can keep us on both paths—for the long haul and into deep time.

Chapter Six

JESUS' UNIQUE ASSAULT ON THE SYSTEMS OF THIS WORLD

When religion is not about healing, it really does not have much to offer people except something later. Many have called it "carrot on the stick" theology. Or as my friend Brian McLaren says, we made the Gospel largely into "an evacuation plan for the next world." If you don't understand the need and desire for the healing of people at many levels, then salvation (*salus* = healing) largely becomes a matter of hoping for some delayed gratification later, which is almost exactly what has happened. And even worse, you surely do not see it as important to heal groups, institutions, the wounds of war, marriage, abuse, race relations, or any of the endless social problems we are drowning in today. Actually, *you no longer know how to* because you never learned the skills at ground zero, the individual human heart.

Healing was not our job or concern, just maintaining social and church order: the doling out of graces and indulgences (as if that were possible); granting dispensations, annulments, and absolutions, along with the appropriate penalties; keeping people in first marriages at all costs, instead of seeing marriage itself as an arena for growth, forgiveness, and transformation for wife, husband, children, and the whole extended family; and more. In general, we tried to resolve issues of the soul and the Spirit by juridical means, which seldom works, in my opinion.

Our overriding concern is to help people put up with it, make the best of it, and then, of course, pass on the same kind of oppressive behavior to the next generation, because we have not recognized it as a problem—oppression, persecution, and mean-spiritedness. If we are not about naming and healing such parts of ourselves, how would we possibly know how to transform them in culture, nation state, the earth itself, the military, or even within church institutions? We have a lot of lost time to make up for.

In the last chapter, my quick review of early Christianity referred to the emergence of the monks, the early desert fathers and mothers. It is an unexpected and surprising movement, because there is nothing directly in Jesus' teaching that gives you the impression there is supposed to be different levels of his vision of discipleship. We were all called equally to follow him. But we divided into our own class system, some who were supposed to "get it" and take it seriously, and some who are just along for the ride. It is interesting that the very term *layman* or *laywoman* in any field applies to people who don't know anything. There are always the professionals (1 percent) and the others (99 percent)! How can that be true if the Gospel hopes to save the world?

Could meditation/contemplation be the very thing that has the power to both democratize and mature Christianity? It alone does not demand major education, does not need a hierarchy of decision makers, does not need to argue about gender issues in leadership or liturgy, does not need licensed officials for sacraments, does not need preachers and bishops, does not have moralistic membership requirement. It just lives and thrives with dedicated pray-ers who have every chance of becoming healers in their worlds, each according to his or her gift. And let's be very honest, Jesus talked a lot more about praying and healing than any of the above.

As you know, one of Thomas Merton's great complaints in his books was that he told his monastery, in effect, "We are not really contemplatives! We just say a lot of prayers!" (See Richard Rohr, *The Naked Now*, Crossroad, 112.) That probably came as a shock to them (he is still not much loved inside his own monastery), and it's a scandal to us: that most religious orders, even those who use the word *contemplative*, for the most part were no longer trained in the older traditions of wordless prayer or letting go of discursive thought. These people were very often introverts, which is fine, but not of itself holy. Prayer beyond words, prayer as a stance, prayer as an alternative consciousness, pretty much stopped being taught after the dualistic mind of the Reformation and the rational mind of the Enlightenment undid the possibility.

From then on, we instead recited prayers and maybe chanted psalms, and filled in the heart gap with lots of pious devotions. That is fine, but it doesn't necessarily take one to that deeper place of the soul, not does it deeply touch the unconscious—where almost all our wounds and shadow material are hidden. No wonder even prayer did not heal many people, and often religious life was filled with some very neurotic personalities, as we see in the autobiography of Thérèse of Lisieux. The Divine Office, as beautiful as it is, still can keep you largely in your head, your left brain, and your world of good ideas. We can now prove that mere discursive prayer does not access the deeper levels of brain function, but is largely a continuation of our daily dualistic thought patterns.

The Architecture of Religion

The Cleansing of the Temple—Jesus' central condemning action, by him and against him—can be read on many levels, and it should be. Scholars have come to see that this action was far more important than many of us imagined. It is Jesus' last dramatic symbolic move before they kill him, and now we know why.

I want to talk about it here, because the same patterns of meritocracy keep recurring in every age, and I think that it will never change until and unless Christianity begins to emphasize a sincere interior life, a world of grace and mercy, as the *only antidote when religion has become a worthiness contest*. The very architecture and use of the Temple courts will make clear how much of a problem this has been, and how the only way out is to make religion "a house of prayer for all the nations" (Mark 11:17), a place where "the blind and the lame" can come to Jesus and be cured (Matt 21:14). Both of these citations come from the story we call the Cleansing of the Temple, and clearly represent a *replacement theology*: the buying and selling of God must be replaced by prayer and healing. In John's interpretation, the physical building must be replaced by the human body of Christ (John 2:19–21). That's the whole agenda for any "emerging Christianity" or "emerging Church." (See "The Emerging Church," a recorded conference available through the Center for Action and Contemplation in Albuquerque, New Mexico, www.cacradicalgrace.org.)

To begin with, Jesus is saying that the very mentality of the "buying and selling" of God or love or mercy has to go, or religion will always remain corrupt and immature. Love does not happen that way. Yet that is where we went, as predicted by the Temple itself, largely toward a religion of subtle but real buying and selling where we, the clergy, became the brokers of worthiness and unworthiness, and controlled the membership requirements of who was in and who was out. This pattern is not unique to Christianity. Hinduism has its caste systems, Buddhism has its upper-class monasteries, and Islam is divided both in terms of gender and of office. But in Judaism, which for me is archetypical religion, it is all mapped out in the very architecture of the Temple itself. In my opinion, what happened to the Temple in Jerusalem is an exact prediction and preparation for what every religion on some level does when it does not go deep, but merely remains concerned with externals, rituals, and boundary markers.

First of all, at the physical center of the Temple, you have the holy of holies, where the high priest can enter one day a year, the Day of Atonement. He is the worthiest of all, as it were. Then outside this, you have the first court of the priests and Levites, and the second court for circumcised Jewish men. Then there is the third court, separated by a grate, which is the court of the Jewish women. This pattern was sometimes replicated in local synagogues at that time, which you have perhaps seen in some biblical movies. Women, at least in their fertile years, were lucky to get in one week out of the month because of the debt codes and purity codes surrounding menstruation, labor, and child-birth, all of which made them "impure" for a certain amount of days. We non-Jews or Gentiles were of course forbidden to go beyond the outer or fourth court, under the pain of death. There was a clear sign to that effect, and scholars wonder if that is exactly what Jesus is criticizing when he says, "My house shall be called a house of prayer for *all* the nations" (Mark 11:17).

Do you really think all this division came from God? That God has divided up Judaism into degrees of worthiness? And to deliberately separate Jews from the rest of God's people? You would think that monotheists would be the first to move beyond such a mentality.

If this isn't bad enough, you also have seven distinct groups declared by the Book of Leviticus that must remain totally outside the Temple as impure or "structurally" sinful. That means about 99.9 percent of all the people God ever created are of no serious interest to their Creator. But before we laugh at their notion of the non-Jewish, the *goyim*, which is us: when I was growing up, we called some of *you* "non-Catholics"! Do you see any pattern here? Religious marginalization, classism, or segregation is especially dangerous because it pretends to come from God. You could write an entire tragic and violent history of the world simply through this single dark lens.

I will list here the seven clear groups who could not enter any court. Without this knowledge you cannot appreciate many New Testament stories, or even get their major point.

1. Those with any kind of contagious disease or skin disease were impure and were lumped under the term *leper*. Anything that was visible on the outside was deemed to be a punishment from God and a sign of impurity.
2. The bastard sons and daughters of priests were impure, as were illegitimates in general.
3. People with any visible handicap or disfigurement were impure, which explains most of Jesus' healing stories.
4. All women after their menstruations and childbirths were impure.

5. Men with injured genitals were impure; this probably included what we would call all people with ambiguous genitalia, hermaphrodites, and eunuchs.

6. Structural, or contextual, "sinners" were impure. These were people whose very occupation put them in touch with dead bodies, impure animals, or the impure substances listed in Leviticus and Numbers; also all cooperators with Judaism's oppressors, for example, tax collectors; and, practically speaking, anyone who was presumed not to conform to rules of ritual cleanliness and required temple visits, like shepherds who lived at a distance from synagogue or temple. Sinfulness was much more a class, a category, a state, an occupation than our later notion of internal attitudes and personal malice, which notion largely comes from Jesus himself! We cannot underestimate how Jesus liberated our notion of what sin might actually be.

7. Gentiles—that is, the other 99 percent of the rest of the world—were variously considered impure, infidels, pagans, lost, and even of the devil.

Now before you get too dismissive of our Jewish friends, remember that many of us grew up with the Catholic communion rail where only the altar boys and the clergy, except the nuns when they cleaned the altar, could come to the other side. The Anglicans solidified this pattern in most English cathedrals: altar, sanctuary, clergy seating, boys' choir, choir, chancel, before we get to the 99 percent of the Christian community. You need a verger to make your way through it all. I once attended an early morning feast day Mass at an unnamed English cathedral, and all these inner courts were filled with highly vested individuals, with a full organ, and a stately procession in and out— while I sat in the front pew all alone. The wonderful woman priest addressed her whole sermon just to me, it seemed. I felt both very special and very sad.

Nowadays, churches are being built as a circle where there is a more inclusive and inviting sense of community. But it has taken us a long time to get there because, basically, we have made religion into a purity contest, and worship spaces usually come to mirror and define that. Once you make the Gospel into a worthiness system, you will create the very things Jesus assaults most in his ministry, but you will also find something very appealing to the ego, which loves such things. The ego/flesh will create a subtle, or not so subtle, list of what we call debt codes and purity codes to decide who is in and who is out. These usually have much more to do with cultural fears, biases, and class judgments than anything that actually keeps us from God or leads us to God. But it feels clear, clean, and somehow just, except to people like Jesus.

Jesus turned these debt and purity codes on their head with his constant touching and consorting with the impure, the sinners, and the outsiders. It actually takes obstinacy *not* to see this. Jesus' affirmation of, and choice for, those in the outer courts is in almost every Gospel story. His criticism of the inner court is also clear and even damning. If you can hear that, you will never read the Gospels the same again, and you will wonder why you did not see it before. It comes down to this, which we can now prove scientifically: people cannot see what they are not told to look for or to expect, or if all quietly agree on a common, usually harmless, domesticated interpretation. *What you decide to see also determines what you do not see.*

After you have read the Gospels for a while, you begin to wonder what Jesus did from Sunday to Thursday. He always seems to wait until Friday evening to Saturday evening to do anything. What is wrong with him? Is he lying in a hammock all week? Well, it is called provocation. He goes out of his way to do his big actions on the Sabbath, and he uses it as an example. How did we not see that? Remember, the Sabbath, along with circumcision and the purity codes, was the primary public boundary marker and loyalty symbol of Judaism in his time. Jesus refuses to be bound by a merely legalistic or ritualistic understanding of his religion. That we could take Jesus of Nazareth and make his teaching into a moral matter instead of a mystical matter is to almost entirely miss the entire thrust of his reform and invitation. Once more, what you decide to look at determines what you do not look at.

Personal versus Corporate Reform

The mainline church largely organized itself around structural charity and almsgiving from our position of security, which is partially necessary and understandable. But what was lost was that deeper sense of solidarity, justice, simplicity, and basic understanding of the situation of the poor ourselves. No longer were we called to become poor like Christ but simply to help the poor through charity. It became okay to get rich personally, including the clergy. But as good as charity is, it largely became an avoidance of a basic concern for justice.

We must realize that this was a step or two removed from what Jesus lived and invited us into. We are no longer the poor whom Jesus called blessed; from our position of comfort, we take care of the poor. This is good and necessary, but not exactly what he suggested.

Even though the Catholic Church wasn't a church *of* the poor, it sometimes became a church *for* the poor, usually through those specialized groups called the religious orders. You could pretty much chart the foundation of two-thirds of the religious orders of the Catholic Church to these wonderful women and men who would see poor boys who were not being taught, poor girls who were not being protected, poor orphans who were not being taken care of. Then one heroic Irish woman would go off and take care of them, and soon you have the Sisters of Mercy, thousands of them.

I'm convinced that *structurally* one of the only reasons Roman Catholicism has lasted is because we have these satellites of freedom on the edge and on the side—the Benedictines, Jesuits, Salesians, and Sisters of Charity and Mercy who aren't that much under the thumb of the whole pyramid. They are just doing their job, and every now and then they salute the bishop when he comes by. You can live in our community of Franciscans for six months and not even hear mention of the bishop. I don't mean that disrespectfully; the role is just not that interesting to us. He has questions he is concerned with, and we have other questions, as do most of the laity. Structurally, I believe, the church survived because the religious orders and most of the laity just got on with trying to live the Gospel, as have many diocesan priests and bishops, too.

The fruit of meditation is that we also ask *new* questions, not in reaction, not in rebellion, not in opposition to religion or the church, not in any sort of negativity. We don't have time for that. It's a waste of your life to bother with any kind of oppositional or negative energy, because soon it becomes another form of righteousness and that would be the death of your contemplative life.

I think we need to ask questions rather than to have answers; we need to just do the job rather than seek the role and office to do it. Now some of us call this utterly new notion of church reformation "emerging Christianity." We do not react, or leave and form a new group, which forces us into untrue dualistic thinking, forces us into wasting time proving the old group was totally wrong and our new group is totally right. We have had 500 years of this, with an awful lot of bad fruit. So now we hope to keep one foot in our historic denomination and tradition, grateful for all it gave us, but we put the other foot in prayer groups, service groups, support groups, mission groups, and meditation groups. That is a rather creative, positive, and hopeful way of renewing the church. No longer seeking to be right, but just getting down to the practical work of our own transformation and the transformation of our suffering world.

Francis knew that you would never reform the church by any frontal attack, by a verbal or theoretical attack. He came, instead, from beneath and from the side and below— and from the positive. He simply lived in a different and more attractive way. He didn't get into oppositional energy. If you go to Assisi today, you can see that he went outside the walls, rebuilt little tiny churches and did it in a way that was beautiful, loving, and positive. We have now taken this as one of our core principles in our Center in New Mexico: "The best criticism of the bad is the practice of the better."

Chapter Seven

A CONTEMPLATIVE STANCE

Perhaps like me, you feel that the longer you live, the more you are forced to ask the question, "What makes people so unkind to one another?" What creates mean-spirited people who want to hurt you or others in even subtle ways? Sometimes the more petty and unnecessary it is, the more astounding it is. Where does this come from? Why is it much easier for humans to wrap themselves around problems, negativity, and blaming than around joy? It is so strange. Even Peter, the symbol for the church, enters the tomb on Easter morning, sees, and says nothing (John 20:6–10). His fear overcomes any possible release to joy or even hope. The passage ends by simply saying the disciples went home again, back to their dreariness, I guess.

You see, humans make hard and impossible the very things they most want. Such contrariness must be the meaning of any original wound or "sin." We really are our own worst enemy. It is not just that we send our unresolved pain and fear toward others, but we choose to abide in it ourselves. We refuse resurrection on a rather regular basis, and then wonder why we are unhappy. Maybe we just need to be told how deep and hidden the problem is, and that *there is another way*. That is what we will try to do here.

Mean-spiritedness and hate appear in some way to be helpful, believe it or not. Any negativity works in a lot of immediate and seemingly good ways. It unites a fear-based group very quickly, far more quickly than love, especially if you do not recognize or admit your own fears. Fear is a well-hidden, denied, and disguised demon. It was the last and latest of the capital sins to be named by the tradition, and it was only the Enneagram that exposed it as probably the capital sin of half of the human race! (There are any number of excellent books on the Enneagram. I personally like *The Wisdom of the Enneagram* by Don Riso and Russ Hudson.)

Fear also unites the disparate parts of your own false self very quickly. Remember, *the ego moves forward by contraction, self-protection, and refusal.* Sad to say, contraction gives you focus, purpose, direction, superiority, and a strange kind of security. It takes your aimless anxiety, covers it up, and tries to turn it in purposefulness and urgency, which shows itself in a kind of drivenness. But this drivenness is not peaceful, it is not happy, it is "filled with itself," as we say. It is filled with agenda and sees all of its problems as "out there." Never "in here."

The soul, however, does not proceed by contraction but by expansion. It moves forward not by exclusion but by inclusion. It sees things deeply and broadly, not by saying *no*, but by saying *yes*, at least on some level, to whatever comes its way. Can you feel those two very different movements within yourself? You must not take my word for it: you must see this for yourself and within yourself, or you will never be able to move beyond it. Just know that Mary's kind of *yes* does not come easily to us. It always requires that you let down some of your ego boundaries, and none of us likes to do that.

When *yes* is asked of us, it will usually be resisted by an attack of anxiety, excuse, rationalization, or question. We must learn how to recognize our own patterns and the exact shape of our fear. "What is your name?" Jesus asks the Gerasene demoniac (Luke 8:30). You cannot exorcise a demon until you know its exact "name," as it were, and until it shows itself; in present psychological language, we would say until the "demon" is pulled out of its hiding place in the unconscious and looked at consciously and nondefensively. Some of us call this "shadow work."

Contraction allows you to eliminate another person, write them off, exclude them, torture them, at least in your mind, and somehow expel them. This immediately gives you a sense of being in control and having a secure set of boundaries, even holy boundaries as the Pharisee was seeking when he said, "God, I thank you that I am not like other people: thieves, rogues, adulterers, or even like this tax collector" (Luke 18:11). Hatred or mean-spiritedness gives one a superior sense of identity, even if it is totally untrue, as Jesus says in this story. It seems that we would sooner have a negative identity than no identity at all.

Unless there is someone to hold us and accompany us on these inner journeys, much of humanity cannot and will not go inside. If only they knew "*Who*" they would meet there, and could say with St. Catherine of Genoa, "My deepest me is God!" Without such accompaniment, most will stay on the surface of their own lives; there, mean-spiritedness is the best boundary and protection from being bothered by others. But with such accompaniment, they will literally "find their souls" and the One who lovingly dwells there.

Hatred is a false way of taking away the doubt and free-floating anxiety that comes with the fragility of human existence. Any negative focus takes away existential angst by giving us a *false* place to stand, but the payoff is that it makes us feel both superior and in control. Hate settles the dust and ambiguity that none of us like. Hate is much more common than love, I am afraid, and seems much more effective. Hate makes the world go round much more than love. Just read the morning paper of any country; it's largely about who is hating, attacking, accusing, stealing from, or exposing whom. It would not even make news to have a headline saying, "Jane Smith is filled with joy today!" We would not find it interesting and would probably not even believe it.

You could say that Jesus came to reveal and resolve this central and essential problem. I consider it the very meaning of the Risen Christ. There is really no other way to save us from ourselves and from each other until we are saved from our need to fear and hate. The pattern is so deep and daily within humans that we even make religion into a cover for our need to be fearful and hateful. I recently had a picketer outside a conference where I was a speaker. He was wearing a big cross, and shouting with venom to all visitors, and then to my face he shouted, "I hate you for listening to these Catholic heretics." Thank God he did not know I was the speaker, or I would have gotten it worse. The ultimate disguise whereby you can remain a mean-spirited person is to do it to for God or country. You are relieved of all inner anxiety; you can maintain your positive self-image and even some kind of moral high ground, while underneath are "the bones of the dead" (Matt 23:27), as Jesus said. This is what Scott Peck called "people of the lie," from his book of the same title. He told me once that personally he thought that was the most important of his books, but it was one of the weakest in sales. The book hit us all below the belt.

We have had so much utopian talk about Jesus and love, but Jesus had a very hard time getting to the issue of love. First he had to expose and destroy the common phenomenon of hate and even fear-hate religion, which I think is the meaning of the cross. Once he exposed the lie of hatred and the illusion it created, love could show itself clearly, but until then it largely couldn't. The pattern is still the same. As Jesus shockingly put it in several places, Satan is the real "ruler of this world" (John 14:30). Hate and fear, it seems, are the ordinary daily agenda. Love is the totally enlightened, entirely nonsensical way out of this daily and ordinary agenda. Love has to be worked toward, received, and enjoyed by, first of all, facing our capacity for fear and hate. But remember, we gather around the negative space quickly, while we "fall into" love rather slowly and only with lots of practice at falling.

Jesus Crucified

The Gospel presents this monstrous dilemma in a personal and cathartic narrative that grounds the whole issue in history and in one man's enlightened response to the human patterns. It starts with one man, Jesus, accepting the religious and social judgment of the hate of his society; "negative unanimity around one," as René Girard calls it. Most of us call it scapegoating. That is why it is so emphasized in the Gospel that we have both church and state—both Caiaphas and Pilate, Jerusalem and Rome—bringing Jesus to his death. Both major power systems declare him to be unworthy, dangerous, and a sinner. The One we believe to be the most perfect person who ever lived is judged by power at the highest levels to be in fact the problem! The passion accounts in the New Testament show you forever how wrong power and authority can be, how incorrect their filters can be. It makes most religious people's love affair with top-down authority rather strange and hard to understand.

Jesus bears the consequences of hatred publicly but in an utterly new way of forgiveness and letting go, which we finally call "resurrection," not just for him but for all of history. A new and possible storyline is set forth. Jesus thus transforms the pattern and creates for us the possibility of seeing even the worst things in a new way. You could say it made the worst thing, the "murder of God," into the very best thing, the redemption of the world. For two thousand years, Jesus has remained the most striking icon of a possible new agenda. His death exposed the lie and the problem as never before. *Jesus was not changing the Father's mind about us; he was changing our mind about the Father—and thus about one another.* If God or Jesus is not hateful, violent, punitive, torturing, or vindictive, then our excuse for the same is forever taken away from us. (Of course, if God is punitive and torturing—as we often perceive him to be— then we have full permission, which is largely what has happened, I am sad to say.)

Jesus' entire journey told people two major things: that life could have a positive story line, and that God was far different, and far better, than they ever thought. He did not just give us textbook answers from a distance, but personally walked through the process of being both rejected and forgiving, and then said, *"Follow me."* This is something you can know only by being in that position and coming out even more alive on the other side. It can't be done theoretically or by a mere theological affirmation.

In meditation, we see such things, and weep ahead of time, before we act on them—or let them act on us. That is much of the message of this whole book. We need a very "practical practice," or all this will remain mere interesting ideas that we will soon forget, nor will there be any real transformation of individuals or of our society.

Sometimes it looks like it is control that is behind hatred, but even control freaks are usually afraid of losing something. If we go deeper into ourselves, we will see that there is both a rebel and a dictator in all of us, two different ends of the same control spectrum. It is almost always fear that justifies our knee-jerk rebellion or our need to dominate, a fear that is hardly ever recognized as such because we are into acting out and trying to control the situation from either the Left or the Right. Either can be, and often is, a mere ego position. Both positions are afraid of losing their control or their power.

As Paul says: "The angels of darkness must always disguise themselves as angels of light" (2 Cor 11:15; my translation). For fear to survive, it has to look like reasonableness, prudence, common sense, intelligence; like the need for social order, morality, religion, obedience, or even justice and spirituality. It usually works: just give your fear a nice cover, and you don't have to face that, underneath, you are afraid of losing something. It might take a while to recognize what that something is. This recognition is called the "discernment of spirits" and is listed as one of the major, needed charisms for the upbuildiing of the Body of Christ (1 Cor 12:10). It has seldom been seriously taught, except by the Jesuits, because we thought that Law and obedience to Law could resolve all spiritual problems. Someday the church will know that you cannot deal with spiritual things juridically. Paul wrote two entire letters, Romans and Galatians, largely addressing this very issue, but with little effect on Catholic history.

You need the discernment of spirits to know the difference between what is apparently happening, or plausibly happening, and what is really happening. It is indeed a charism, and needs to be compassionately taught. For example, we can call something "justice" while we really mean and fully intend vengeance. But the word *justice* sounds good. You hear such misuse of words on the news every night. One wonders if the inner need to punish the other, to hurt the other, has ever been faced or ever been recognized? When someone has made you afraid, you want to hurt them back or at least diminish them in some way.

The charism of the discernment of spirits is taught and followed by Jesus himself in the telling accounts of his temptations in the desert (Matt 4:1–11). He had to face his own potential for evil, for selfishness, for power, before he could name it or exorcise it in others. If we pretend the demon is not within us, we will never be a good healer or "exorcist." We will almost always *project what we refuse to see in ourselves onto others.* And please do not call this "mere psychology," for all you need to do is read Jesus' teaching on the splinter in your neighbor's eye and the log in our own, and you will see he is making the exact same point (Matt 7:1–5). Jesus was really quite psychologically sophisticated, or, better, he was just in touch with universal wisdom.

If you want to see splinters and logs, try sitting every morning and every evening for at least twenty minutes. If anybody thinks we are waiting for ecstasy, know that it is invariably twenty minutes of dying! In fact, if you are not learning to let go, but you are still wrapping yourself around your opinions and solidifying your righteousness, then you are not meditating. Any contemplative practice is a daily withdrawing of projections, denials, and infatuations. It is shadowboxing without end and is nothing less than hard work. As Buddhist teacher Jack Kornfeld put it, the occasional moment of union or enlightenment is always followed by the ordinary: "After the ecstasy, the laundry"! (This is from his book of the same name.)

To be trapped inside your own small ego, small self, is always to be afraid, always to seek some kind of control. To not have Anyone that you can trust deeply is necessarily to be a control freak. Thus, great religion tries to free individuals from the tyranny of their small and fragile selves and introduce them to Someone-They-Can-Trust. Only if you trust such a Someone will you eventually know that you do not have to create all the patterns, and you do not have to solve all the problems. *You are being guided.*

You do not have to explain all the failures, or take responsibility for all the fixing. Finally you know you are a part of the general dance. What else would be the beginnings of peace? As long as you think you've got to fix everything and control everything and explain everything and understand everything, you will never be a peaceful person. Note that these things largely happen by endless ruminating in the mind. The Enneagram taught many of us that "fear people" are "head people," which was a great surprise to most folks. Our common phrase "peace of mind" is a complete misnomer. When you are in your mind, you are never at peace, and when you are at peace—take note—you are never in your head, but in a much larger Unified Field.

The Scapegoat Mechanism

The process of both denying and projecting your fears and hates elsewhere is called, as we said earlier, "scapegoating." The strange word I think come from the King James Bible, where instead of speaking of the "escaping goat," they translated it as "scapegoat," and now it has become our English word. In Leviticus 16, the ritual of the scapegoat is described in great detail. As ritual, it had genius; we would perhaps call it ritual confession today. On the Day of

Atonement, the high priest laid all the sins of the people from the past year on a select goat, and then with reeds the people beat him out into the desert. And apparently it worked, just as it has in most of history.

So what we now call scapegoating is seeing this same ritual process in human affairs. One could, without much exaggeration, say that it is the storyline of most of human history. If the problem of ignorant and violent killing is, in fact, the problem at the heart of humanity, you can perhaps see why the "Savior of the world" (John 4:42) would come in this form, revealing both the problem and the correct answer in his final act on Calvary.

History up to now has largely been the story of who killed whom and why, and then afterward, the eventual exposing that the reasons were false or misused. The scapegoat mechanism is almost entirely hidden in the unconscious; it proceeds from our denied but real need to project our anxiety elsewhere. Unfortunately, there is no *elsewhere* in the spiritual world. *Meditation is refusing to project our anxieties elsewhere, and learning to hold and face them within myself and within God.*

Do you know that the very name *Satan* means the "accuser"? Watch for the accusing spirit within yourself. Notice that, if there is any free-floating anxiety within you, you will always want to think negative thoughts about somebody else. It must be hard to be married because there is a projection screen very close at hand. There he or she is lying right next to you: a very easy target.

I can certainly make one absolute statement: *In the spiritual life, we are always our own primary problem.* I, myself, wish that it were not true. It is almost a sign of a transformed person when they can face the often painful paradox of their existence like Jesus faced it on the cross. As my paraphrase to Paul's Letter to the Romans says: "He became the problem to overcome the problem" (8:3). Jesus didn't project the problem on to any other group, race, religion, homosexual, or abortionist; he held it and suffered it and thus transformed it into major medicine for the world. That is the redemptive pattern in one clear statement. We sometimes refer to it as the "third way," or the "paschal mystery." If you are called to help homosexuals or work for a pro-life world, you cannot begin to do it until you face head-on your own fears, prejudices, and angers in regard to these issues. Otherwise, you will be more a part of the problem yourself, than a healer for anybody. One of the main reasons I founded the Center to teach activists the contemplative mind was because I saw this problem just about everywhere, and with both conservatives and liberals.

The significance of Jesus' wounded body is his deliberate and conscious holding of the pain of the world and refusing to send it elsewhere. *The wounds were not necessary to convince God that we were loveable; the wounds are to convince us of the path and the price of transformation.* They are what will happen to you if you face and hold sin in compassion instead of projecting it in hatred. Jesus' wounded body is an icon for what we are all doing to one another and to the world. Jesus' resurrected body is an icon of God's response to our crucifixions. The two images contain the whole message of the Gospel.

Jesus agrees to be the Wounded One, and we Christians are these strange believers in a wounded healer. If I were to name the Christian religion, I would probably call it the "Way of the Wound." We come to God not through our strength, but through our weakness. We learn wisdom and come to God not by doing it all right, nearly as much as we learn about doing it all wrong. Our Jesus is a victim before he is a victor, and on some level we are, too. Who would have thought?

If any of you were going to create a religion, who of you would think of creating as your religious image a naked, bleeding, wounded man? It is the most unlikely image for God; the most illogical image for Omnipotence. None of us in our wildest imagination would have come up with it. It must be exposing a very central issue, a very central problem for God to come into the world in this form and in this way. We Christians have now become accustomed to it, perhaps we have domesticated it, and we no longer receive the shock and the scandal of all that it is saying.

Scapegoating works so well, there is no likely reason to think it is going to end or change. Until you are enlightened by grace, you don't even see it; it remains safely hidden in the unconscious where it plays itself out. There is a Gospel passage that has been very little preached on and hardly ever commented on. It says, "When the unclean spirit has gone out of a person, it wanders...looking for a resting place, but it finds none. Then it says, 'I will return to my house from which I came'" (Matt 12:43–44). There is the unconscious pattern described almost perfectly. Rather than have my self-doubt or my self-hatred come home to roost, we make sure it finds a resting place somewhere else. Once you spot and stop the pattern, the game is over, but you have to let the unclean spirit return to "your own house," as it were. The cross of Jesus was a mirror held up to history, so some at least could spot and stop the pattern.

Only the great self, the True Self, the Godself, can carry such anxiety. The little self can't do it. People who don't pray basically can't live the Gospel because the self is not strong enough to hold the anxiety and the fear. I'm most quoted for this line: "*If you do not transform your pain, you will always transmit it.*" Always someone else has to suffer because *I* don't know how to suffer; that's what it comes down to. Jesus, you could say, came to show us how to suffer, how to carry "the legitimate pain of being human," as C. G. Jung called it. Watch for any spirit of accusation; as soon as it comes, mistrust it; usually you are running from yourself and your own legitimate suffering.

Some have said that the best we have been able to do in the last forty years is to move hatred to ever higher forms of sophistication and ever more subtle forms of disguise, but we still love to hate: Feminists can hate men, liberals can hate conservatives; activists can hate rich people, good family-values folk can hate homosexuals, and victims can hate perpetrators.

To use a metaphor, most people are like electric wires: what comes in is what goes out. Someone calls you a name, and you call them a name back; that is, most people pass on the same energy that is given to them. Now compare an electric wire to those big ugly grey transformers that you see on telephone poles. Dangerous current or voltage comes in, but something happens inside that gray box and what comes out is, in fact, now helpful and productive.

When you see transformers on telephone poles from now on, think of Jesus. That is what he did: he hung on the cross, and the energy that came toward him, he did not return in kind. He held it inside, and made it into something much better that would now pass through history. He is our new and pure electric current. He is not paying any price to God, as if God need to be talked into loving God's creation. Jesus is paying a price to the soul—so that we can see! That is how "he took away the sin of the world." He refused to pass it on! Until the world understands that, there will be no new world.

A Bit of History

In the thirteenth century, the Franciscans and the Dominicans were the church's debating society, as it were. We were allowed to have minority positions in those day, which makes me think we have moved backward. We invariably took opposing positions in the great debates in the universities of Paris, Cologne, and Oxford, and neither opinion was kicked out of the church in those days. One of the debates was on St. Anselm's famous and influential writing, *Cur Deus Homo?* ("Why did God become a human being?").

St. Thomas Aquinas and the Dominicans were being true to the Scriptures, many of which give you the impression that a ransom has to be paid to someone, and that atonement has to be made to God. They were just being faithful to Jewish temple metaphors of sacrifice, price, and atonement. But our Franciscan teacher Blessed John Duns Scotus, who established the theological chair at Oxford, said that Jesus wasn't solving any problems with God. *Jesus wasn't changing God's mind about us but, rather, he was changing **our** mind about God.* Scotus built his argument much more on Colossians' and Ephesians' understanding of the preexistent Cosmic Christ. Jesus is "the image of the invisible God," who came forward in a moment of time so we could look upon "the One we have pierced" and see God's unconditional love—and at the same time see what humans do to almost everything—and then witness God and Jesus' unconditional love-response to that.

The image of the cross was to change us, not to change God, and so Scotus concluded that Jesus' incarnation and death were not at all necessary: Jesus was a pure gift, and the realm of gift is much better than the realm of necessity. We were not saved because of any problem whatsoever, or to pay any debt to devil or to God, but purely to reveal to the soul Divine Love. As usual, the Franciscans were right, but unfortunately we lost the debate, and the mainline Dominican position has been held by most Catholics and Protestants to this day, with a lot of sad results. Someone called it "the most unfortunately successful piece of Christian theology ever written," because it implied that God was not naturally and unconditionally in love with what God created.

Chapter Eight

FINDING OUR CHARISM

Night is our diocese and silence is our ministry
Poverty our charity and helplessness our tongue-tied
    sermon.
Beyond the scope of sight and sound we dwell
    upon the air
Seeking the world's gain in an unthinkable
    experience.
We are exiles in the far end of solitude, living as
    listeners
With hearts attending to the skies we cannot
    understand:
Waiting upon the first far drums of Christ the
    Conqueror,
Planted like sentinels upon the world's frontier.

—Thomas Merton

When I read this section of the Thomas Merton poem "The Quickening of St. John the Baptist" (*The Collected Poems of Thomas Merton*, New Directions, 201), I think of people who meditate. I think of what Christian contemplatives have taken upon themselves, "planted like sentinels upon the world's frontiers," doing something that, frankly and unfortunately, will never fill stadiums. To meditate daily, morning and evening, is to have chosen, accepted, and surrendered to a vocation. We must think of it that way. It is a vocation that places you at the center of history and yet also at its very edge, because most will see you as innocuous, pious, or maybe even self-centered. That poverty might well be our deepest charity, Merton seems to say. They, most people, won't know that you are holding it all together, that you are the microcosmic moment that somehow hears, re-creates, allows, and passes on "the first far drums of Christ the Conqueror."

I have tried to talk about the place to stand; about the True Self, the integrated self; about the big vision, the big picture that we try to hold together; but I haven't talked much about the lever. Maybe I have hesitated to do that because I don't believe there is just one lever; I believe there are many. As Paul so beautifully says, placing all our gifts inside of one great trinitarian flow: "Now there are varieties of gifts, but the same Spirit; and there are varieties of services, but the same Lord; and there are varieties of activities, but it is the same God who activates all of them in everyone" (1 Cor 12:4–7). Paul almost sees us together as a "fourth presence" in the Holy Trinity, invited into the Divine Dance that is God. (See Richard Rohr, "The Divine Dance," and Cynthia Bourgeaul, "The Shape of God," recorded conferences available through the Center for Action and Contemplation in Albuquerque, New Mexico, www.cacradical grace.org.)

It seems to me much of the proper work of the church should be the discerning and empowering of gifts among the people of God and for the world. This would reflect stage 2's illuminative way of spirituality and would get us beyond endless stage 1 moralizing, or the purgative way. There doesn't seem to be much discernment, even in seminaries or chancery offices, whether a person really has a gift. It becomes too often mere church careerism or the filling of slots instead of actual prayerful discernment of *whether one actually has the gift*, for example, of leading, reconciling, healing, preaching, administrating, or counseling. These "free gifts"—as opposed to offices, roles, or something one is merely educated into—are called "charisms" by St. Paul. (See much of chapters 12 and 13 of First Corinthians.)

Most of us who are ordained had to discover if we actually had any charisms only after we were ordained. How strange that most of us were sent out to lead people to faith, hope, and love had no actual track record of ever once doing that? (I was a shy, young friar and never in my wildest dreams imagined I would one day be listened to or read.) How painful it has been for those who were not perhaps gifted in preaching, and yet had to stand up and preach week after week; or for those who have no gift for wisdom or counseling or healing, and yet had people put their lives trustfully in their hands. Untold damage has been done because we let office, role, title, vestment, and formal ordination try to substitute for the free gifts of God. It is almost as if we could not trust that such gifts could or would be given, and then *we ended up not seeing them where they really were*—often in women, simple workers, those outside our denomination, the uneducated, and so on. You could say that we tried to create gifts where they were not, and we refused to see them where they were: "He is a Catholic bishop and therefore automatically a doctor in divinity," or, "She is an Evangelical laywoman who cannot possibly have any gift of healing."

I am convinced that the Book of Jonah can best be read as God moving someone from a mere religious job, role, or career to an actual sense of personal call or destiny, or what

I called earlier one's delivery system. It takes being "swallowed by a beast" and taken into a dark place of nesting and nourishing that normally allows you to move to that deeper place called *personal vocation*. You could describe it as *moving from being ego driven to being soul drawn*. The energy is very different. It comes quietly and generously from within you, and you do not look for payment, reward, or advancement because you have found your soul gift. You have to do it, or you are not you!

I have met many people like this, and they are always a joy to work with. You can tell they are not counting the cost, but just want to serve and help however they can. Benedictines have a lay group that they call "Oblates," which means "those who are offered." To come with your life as a free and given offering is quite different from the seeking of a career, or of any kind of security or status or title. Even the Vatican office for bishops dared to admit publicly a few years ago that they were worried about the rampant careerism among bishops worldwide: the seeking of promotion to higher and more prestigious dioceses. It sounds like we still have James and John wanting to sit at the right and left sides of the throne of Jesus. Maybe the young man or woman sometimes starts there, but you see why Jonah then has to be shoved out of the boat, or he will never get to the "right" Nineveh.

Meditation should lead to a clarity about what you are and maybe even more, *what you are not*. I have found it difficult over the years to sit down and tell people what is *not* their gift; it is usually very humiliating for the person. One sometimes wonders where such illusion and entitlement come from, even among very nice people. I guess we are not a truth-speaking people, we don't speak the truth to one another, nor does our culture encourage the journey toward the True Self.

So the false self often sets itself up for unnecessary failures and humiliations. Just watch the auditions for the TV show *American Idol* sometime. Or better, don't watch the auditions for *American Idol*! That so much *certainty* of a special talent can coexist with so much *lack* of any actual talent really defies analysis. One wonders if these people have any truly loving friends who would tell them the truth. But if it is true in the church, it is because it is true in the whole culture too.

So I ask you to listen, wait, and pray for your charism. Most of us are really only good at one or two things. In general, I have said to social ministry groups that I think there are three basic levels of social ministry, and none is better than the other.

1. At the first level, we pick drowning people out of the swollen stream, dealing with the immediate social problem right in front of us: a man who comes to your door and says he is hungry, and you give him a sandwich or even invite him inside. These are hands-on ministries, social service ministries, like the proverbial soup kitchen. Such works will always look rather generous, Christian, and charitable, and tend to be admired if not always imitated. America is now second to last on the list of industrialized nations in offering charity to the rest of the world. This first level does not take a lot of formal education, usually just a big heart, and a ready gift of your time and often money.

2. At the second level, there are ministries that either help people not to fall into the swollen stream in the first place, or show them how to build their own canoe and to paddle well. In general, these are the ministries of education and healing. Most of the religious orders in the last three hundred years went in that direction, sometimes to the neglect of the other two levels. That is why we filled our country with primary schools and hospitals, universities and technical programs, whereby we could help people who were going to fall into the swollen stream, give them the skills so they wouldn't fall in, or show them survival skills if they ever did. These are ministries that empower you, and give you new visions and possibilities for your own life, for your own dignity. Many religious sisters who once ran our Catholic school systems now have begun to do other forms of education, very often in small or large social service organizations. These folks get little notice and not as much praise now, but they are filling in so many unnoticed gaps, and are surely doing the work of the Gospel. It has to be a deep sense of vocation, because most of them get paid very little.

3. And finally, at what I am going to call the third level, are ministries in building and maintaining the dam that will stop the stream from drowning people in the first place. This is the work of social advocacy, critiques of systems, organization, speeches, boycotts, and

protest and resistance against all forms of
organized injustice and deceit. This level
surely demands the highest level of education
and self-confidence. One has to know how to
access the system, how the system works, and
how to speak the language and understand
the maneuvers of those on the inside. Most
people, frankly, don't feel that kind of call or
have the self-confidence, organization, or
backup to do it, but that does not mean they
do not care about the poor!

More about this last level: it's what people for the last
forty years have called "activism" or "advocacy work." I don't
think most people feel called to activism; I myself don't, even
though I have done my protests in the past. I don't really
believe that is the best way I can serve. Several times in
Washington and Cincinnati I was jailed and led off in my
Franciscan habit. I was making my statement, and hopefully
supporting others; but I had to finally admit that was not
what I was called to do. It was humiliating to limit myself, and
I lost the trust and admiration of some friends and support-
ers. But as we come to know our soul gift more clearly, we
almost always have to let go of some other "gifts" so we can
do our one or two things with integrity, instead of always
being driven by what has been called "the tyranny of the
urgent." Soon urgency is a way of life, and things are not done
contemplatively or peacefully from within. Do one or two
things wholeheartedly in your life: that is all God expects and
all you can probably do well. *Too much good work becomes a
violence to yourself and finally to those around you.*

This third level of social ministry can take the form of
social protest, public resistance, or letter writing—or just

being a gadfly committed to pestering the status quo. Someone had better be doing that. The important thing is that we all should be doing something for the rest of the world. We all have to pay back, particularly those of us born into this rich and comfortable country. We also must respect and support the other two levels, even if you cannot do them. Avoid all comparisons about *better* or *lesser, more committed* or *less committed*: those are all ego games. Let's just use our different gifts to create a unity in the work of service (Eph 4:12), and back one another up, without criticism or competition. Only in our peaceful mutual honoring do we show forth the glory of God. None of us are the whole enchilada! *When justice work is not charity, then it is not true justice. And when charity work does not promote justice, it is not finally charity.*

If you are working on the third level, you won't win a lot of friends. You will have to be ready to bear a lot more criticism at that level because we are not used to social advocacy, even sometimes from people on levels one and two! The church had been so deeply in collusion with the status quo until the 1960s that when the first prophetic voices began to recognize racism or injustice, they were not met with much praise by fellow Christians. It never entered our minds that a Christian was supposed to call the systems of this world into question. We were supposed to be nice. But you know what? The word *nice* is not found in the whole New Testament. The Gospel is not about being nice; it *is* about being honest and just, and the world doesn't like those two things very much. Our job is to learn how to be honest, but with love and respect.

Dr. Martin Luther King, Jr., taught us that, before you go out to witness for justice, you had to make sure in your heart that you could love and respect those who disagreed with you. Can you image the surrender necessary for those who have been oppressed for generations? I don't know how you can surrender to love and respect without some prayer and meditation. How could you go to that deep place where you do not want to publicly expose, humiliate, or defeat your opponents, but rather work, as Martin Luther King said, for win-win situations? To work for win-win solutions, not win-lose, takes a high level of spiritual development, and that is probably why Dr. King's movement didn't go very far and was opposed even by many of his own black people. It demanded in-depth spiritual conversion. The Gospel is not just Leftist politics and protest.

When you are hurt, you want to hurt back; when you are put down by your opponent, you want to put down the opponent. When I founded the Center for Action and Contemplation twenty-four years ago in Albuquerque, it was in response to my first fifteen years on the road. I met so many wonderful social activists. I would agree with their conclusions and with their politics, but to be honest I was often disappointed in their actual energy, sometimes their goals, and often their seeming motivation. They seemed to be as alienated, angry, and negative as the people on the other side of the argument, and I knew that wasn't going to get us anywhere. Ego on the Left is just as problematic and blind as ego on the Right.

So we formed a place that would teach contemplative prayer to activists, to people who were working for social change. In 1986, I was convinced that one half of my teaching would be on social analysis, liberation theology, the biblical tradition of social critique—and the other half would be on contemplative prayer. Twenty-four years later, if you come to our Center today, I think we probably do 80 percent of our teaching on contemplation, and then we find that social critique takes care of itself.

You change sides from **inside**—from the power position to the position of vulnerability and solidarity, which gradually changes everything. Once you are freed from your paranoia, from the narcissism that thinks you are the center of the world, or from your belief that thinks your rights and dignity have to be defended before other people's rights and dignity, then you can finally live and act with justice and truth. Once these blocks are taken away from you—and that is what contemplative prayer does—then you just have to offer a few guiding statements of social analysis and people get it for themselves. *They start being drawn instead of being driven.*

I still think true contemplation is the most subversive of activities because it undercuts the one thing that normally refuses to be undercut—our natural individualism and narcissism. We all move toward the ego, and we even solidify it as we get older if something doesn't expose it for the lie that it is: not because it is bad, but because it thinks it is the whole enchilada! People don't really change too much by themselves; God changes you, if you can expose yourself to God at that level. This is why Christian meditation will never fill stadiums, because not so many people want their narcissism and separateness to be exposed for the silliness that it is.

Eric Erickson, in his analysis of developmental stages, said that if a person doesn't become *generative* somewhere between the ages of fifty and sixty-five, meaning someone who generates life for the next generation and not just for themselves, then they enter into what Erickson called "estrangement." They are foundationally estranged from themselves and the rest of the world as they try to secure their last twenty years around themselves. Let's be honest: we all know a lot of people like that. No one ever told them there was anything more than building their own tower.

Sometimes it might even have been our own fathers and mothers who thought that the final stage of life was about taking care of themselves. One wonders how a culture with so much education, so much opportunity, and so much supposed enlightenment produced so many people who became so petty in their final years. I think they never became generative people because they never heard the Gospel, much less how to internalize it with a real inner life. Maybe you are the one to end that family cycle.

When I am teaching in Europe, I hear again and again from informed people that they expect within thirty years China will be the superpower of the world and not the United States. If so, I don't think that has entered our minds yet; we can't imagine a world where we are not on top. Yet China may well be the superpower of the world, and European countries may well have more Moslems and mosques than Christians and churches in a hundred years. If we are not ready for major economic conversion, some readiness for downward mobility and a big dose of humility, the century ahead will not be a pleasant one. Will believers be in any position to lead the way and set the tone? I hope our prayer practice is preparing us, at least Christians, for just such a future.

Chapter Nine

THE NEED FOR INITIATION

I have found the phenomenon of male initiation in every culture and on every continent until the modern era. (See my book *Adam's Return*, mentioned above.) Something that universal—and so uniform in its goals—was surely fulfilling a deep human and social need. It was deemed necessary for cultural survival, it seems. Initiation is the oldest form of spiritual instruction in the world that we know of and might be called "religion before the great world religions began." Interestingly enough, it was only the male who had to be taught. Women learned in other ways. What we can recognize in intiation is universal patterns of wisdom that needed to be taught to the young male or he was considered useless, dangerous, and a loose cannon in the social fabric. The male, they discovered, would always seek his own power, his own advancement, and his own career at the neglect of just about everybody else. The male is very inclined, it seems, to narcissism, and this had to be exposed, humbled, and turned around into self-confidence, bravery, and perseverance for his wife, his children, and the community. It often does, thank God.

So what initiation did, in the early stages of a young man's "tower-building," was to teach him about a necessary downward journey, so he would remember how and why to make the journey when it was demanded of him, usually later. The major principle was this: *If the male is not led onto journeys of powerlessness, we can assume that he will use, misuse, and abuse his own power for his own purposes.* Before we get defensive, Brothers, just study history, even the history of the church. Is there any other story line? Except for the saints and prophets?

Now, perhaps with that critical insight, we are prepared like never before to understand Jesus' clear and demanding teaching to the twelve men about surrender, the necessity of suffering, humility, servant leadership, and nonviolence. He was initiating them! (Note the significantly different response of the women to both his impending death and to his resurrection). The men resist him every time, and so he finally has to make the journey himself and tell them, "Follow me!" But we avoided that too by making the message into something he never said: "Worship me." Worshipping Jesus is rather harmless and costless now; following Jesus would change everything.

Lenin is supposed to have said shortly before he died, as he became a bit wiser, that if he had to do his Russian revolution over again, he would ask for ten Francises of Assisi instead of more Bolsheviks. He had realized that something imposed by domination and violence from above only creates the same mirrored response from below. It is just a matter of time. He realized that the only communism that would ever be helpful to the world was the voluntary and joyous simplicity of a Francis of Assisi. That clear element of the teaching of Jesus was never taught with any great seriousness. It was never expected of the clergy, certainly not of the higher clergy, and, therefore, why would we, or could we, ask it of the rest of the church? Jesus was training the leaders, because you can only ask of others what you yourselves have done first. Again, he was initiating them as elders, much more than ordaining them as priests (the word is not even used of his disciples).

Once we saw the clerical state as a place of advancement instead of downward mobility, once ordination was not a form of initiation but a continuation of patriarchal patterns, the authentic preaching of the Gospel became the exception rather than the norm—whether Orthodox, Catholic, or Protestant. It became a way to go to heaven later, instead of much interest in changing our lives or our world now.

I have often thought that this "nonpreaching" of the Gospel was like a social contract, as we shake hands across the pulpit. We clergy agree not to tell you anything that would make you uncomfortable, so you will keep coming to our services and paying for our salaries. It is a nice deal, because once we preach the true Gospel, I doubt if you are going to fill the churches. But the discernment and the call to a life of service, to a life that gives itself away instead of simply protecting and procuring for itself in the name of Jesus, is what parishes could still be about. And many are, so we know there has indeed been some preaching and living of the Gospel.

The Necessary Pendulum of History

If we look at history, I think we can see a constant swinging back and forth between two poles, representing two necessary values. Those two necessary values have something to do with the first task of life and the second task of life, but they also need and feed one another.

The first value seeks order, certitude, clarity, and control. It is the best way to start, as we said earlier. But whenever that pattern is in place for too long or is too overbearing, what will always eventually emerge is a critical alternative consciousness. Whenever you overdo the law-and-order thing, you will have another group of people react against it. Once you have an establishment, you will eventually have a *dis*-establishment. When some have all the power, those who don't have power ask very different questions, and the pendulum swings back again—eventually. That has been the story of most of history and the sequencing of most revolutions. It is understandable and predictable, although the extremism on both sides could be avoided if we had more initiated elders who held the middle.

What's interesting to me is that we took the words *Right* and *Left* from the Estates General in France, where on the right of the throne sat the nobility and the clergy (what were we clergy doing over there?), and on the left sat the peasants and 90 percent of the population. Those terms are now commonly used terms in the global political world. The Right is normally concerned for maintaining some status quo, stability, continuity, and authority; that is a legitimate need and without it you have chaos. Without it, you don't know your place to stand. Those on the Right are normally considered innocent until proven guilty. Those on the Left are presumed, for some reason, to be guilty until proven innocent, at least in the minds of many. The powers that be have tended to write history from the side of the victors. Once you see this, you wonder why you never saw it before. But some form of the Right is necessary for authority and continuity in a culture, and some form of the Left is necessary for truth and reform in a culture. And thus the pendulum swings, and I guess we all hope we are living at the appropriate time when it is swinging toward our side!

In the biblical tradition these two poles are symbolized by the kings and the prophets. There is almost a necessary opposition between them. There is only one time in all the

Hebrew Scriptures that those two ever make friends, and then only barely. That is when David the king accepts the critique of Nathan the prophet, after Nathan accuses him of his sinfulness and David has the humility to say that he was correct: "I have sinned against the LORD" (see 2 Sam 12).

The Right always considers itself the product of rationality, experience, and civilization. The people on the Left are always the product of these "silly" people's movements arising out of high-minded ideology, unbearable injustices, or both. These movements are not rational. They are not well planned at the beginning. They are intuitive and come from what's suffered by the little people, who at that point are of no account and have no press or status. Thus they rely on symbols, songs, slogans, and momentary charismatic leaders to get off the ground. Remember when white people laughed at those black people singing "We Shall Overcome"? Now we look back fifty years later and we see how the biblical pattern of Exodus was again revealed, and how Martin Luther King showed all the marks of a biblical prophet, even to the final prediction of his death. He knew where that kind of truth was going to lead him. Yet most Christians could not see this, and many still do not—while saying they love the story of Exodus!

The point is that most of political and church history has been controlled and written by people on the Right because they are the educated people. *One of the few subversive texts in history, believe it or not, is the Bible. The Bible is a most extraordinary text because again and again it legitimates, not the people on the top, but invariably the people on the bottom.* After a while you might get tired of the rejected son, the barren woman, the sinner, always being the chosen one of God! You see their helplessness—and what marvelous symbols of powerlessness they are—and then out of that powerlessness God creates power. It is like the First Step of the Twelve-Step program. The first necessary spiritual step—for all of us, not just addicts—is the realization that we are powerless, and then through our Eleventh Step of "prayer and meditation" we come closer to our Higher Power. If you don't walk through that clarification and conversion, it doesn't happen.

Normally, institution theology is the legitimation of what we are already doing and what we *need* to be true to in order to maintain our institution. For example, at the Council of Trent in 1545, we said there are seven sacraments; that there always were and there always would be. That is patently not true, but that was becoming the Catholic practice at that point. We couldn't back down now in the presence of Martin Luther, so we falsely asserted that we always believed it and that it was always that way. In fact, there were only two sacraments for much of our history, baptism and Eucharist. The history of the sacraments is itself a pendulum swing between the needs of the Left (the laity) and the demands of the Right (the clergy). If the needs of the Left actually won out, I would suspect we would have seventy sacraments instead of seven: like the washing of the feet, forgiveness ceremonies for failed marriages, communal prayer over the sick, liturgies of lament, agape meals, public reconciliation rituals, cleansing of warriors after war, and so on.

Except for the Bible itself, it took till the second half of the twentieth century for the Left to begin to have a public and legitimate voice. I do not think that is an overstatement. In any swing of the pendulum in the direction of justice, the masses, the bottom, were always considered subversive and traitorous, up till the last century. Why not, when even the church was looking down from the top, and the Bible had been made into establishment literature—while it clearly is not. *The Bible affirms law, authority, and tradition, as most writings in most of history have done, but then it does something beyond and more: it affirms reform, change, and the voiceless—and makes them even stronger.* This is what makes the Bible an inspired book. It has guided Western history to this point more than people realize, I believe.

That biblical bias toward the bottom has now been adopted in the new constitutions of 86 percent of the religious orders of the world. You see why I say religious life is an alternative consciousness. The bias has been called by some "the preferential option for the poor." But it *is* an *option*, an *invitation*: it is a grace, and it emerges from inner freedom—or else it would not be from God. Nevertheless, it is clearly the final chosen option of the Bible. In other words, *the Bible is biased*; it takes the side of the rejected ones, the poor ones, the abandoned ones, the barren women, and the ones who have been excluded, tortured, and kept outside, all summed up in Jesus himself. Hard to deny when you think of it.

Perhaps a Surprise

Why does the Bible and why does Jesus tell us to care for the poor and the outsider? *Because we need to stand in that position for our own conversion.* We need to understand the mercy of God, the forgiveness of God, the grace of God. You need it yourself: you yearn for it and you long for it. When you are too smug and content, then grace and mercy have no meaning. Forgiveness is not even desired. When we have pulled ourselves up by our own bootstraps, religion is always corrupted because it doesn't understand the Mystery of how divine life is transferred. How people change. How life flows. It has been said by others that religion is largely filled with people who are afraid of hell, and spirituality is for people who have gone through hell. As all initiation rites say: you have to die before you die and then you know.

Jesus is always on the side of the crucified ones. He changes sides in the twinkling of an eye to go wherever the pain is. He is not loyal to one religion, or this or that group, or the worthy—*Jesus is always loyal to suffering.* Do you realize that takes away all of our usual places to stand? In other words, he is just as loyal to the suffering of Iraqi boys as he is to the suffering of American boys. He is just as loyal to an oppressed gay man as he is to an oppressed married woman. Darn it! He grabs all our boundaries away from us, and suddenly all we have is a free fall into the arms of God, our only security. That is exactly God's agenda, if I am to believe the Bible.

God is on the side of pain wherever the pain is. God is on the side of all human suffering, even the poor young German boys used by the Nazis. And so you see the insanity of war. Whom should I kill when Jesus is everywhere? Try to preempt Jesus now for your own group, religion, or country. Try to justify your just war, and shoot Jesus in that Vietnamese peasant or that Iraqi mother. It is impossible. Jesus is what mythology called a "shape-shifter," and no one seeking power can use him for their private purposes. Those whose hearts are opened to human pain will see Jesus everywhere, and their old dualistic minds will serve them less and less, for the Shape-Shifter ends up shifting our very shape too.

Find me one single healing story in the Gospel where Jesus demands that you belong to his religion, that your first marriage be annulled, that you received the proper sacraments, that you are orthodox (the word is not found in the

Bible), or that your sexual orientation is appropriate. How can we avoid such clear messages? The only and simple prerequisite for the touch and healing of Jesus is desire itself.

The only people who want God's healing are those who have longed for it, whose heart has been emptied out by suffering and pain. They call out, like the little blind man on the road, "Jesus, Son of God, have mercy on me," and Jesus moves right toward them, as he does with all who ask.

We have a lawyer with a bright mind who joined our Franciscan Province. After working in the priesthood for a couple of years, he was sitting with me one day, and he said, "You know, this church is harder and harder for me to understand. We claim to have the perfect medicine, the healing power to restore and renew hearts and souls, but we also always seem to be saying, 'Make sure you don't really need it! Because if you really need it, you are a less than ideal member!' Forgiveness, reconciliation, compassion, and healing are mere concessions to the unfortunate instead of the very path of salvation itself. But in fact, they are very nature of God. *So make sure, make absolutely sure, that you always need them.*"

In the Eucharist, we move beyond mere words and go to that place where we don't talk about the Mystery anymore, we begin to eat it and chew on it. In the Eucharist, we move our knowing to the physical, emotional, and cellular level. I see now that that it is easier for God to convince bread of its sacred identity than it is to convince people. It's easier for God to convince wine of what it is: wine will have no problem knowing that it is the Blood of Christ, but we humans do. So we keep feeding you the bread and wine that believe what they are, who they are—a perfect medicine, you might say. One day it will dawn on your heart, "My God, I am what I eat!" and at last the two presences will have become one Real Presence. The Eucharist is not a reward for good behavior, but medicine and food for sinners and for those who do not know they are the very Body of Christ.

Scientists are now saying that the neural grooves that you prefer and use become ingrained patterns in the brain. If we cease thinking alternatively, then alternative ways of thinking die. And so the neural grooves that you prefer to use take over by the time you're in your forties and fifties, and that is probably why a lot of old people are not very interesting: they have four or five remaining neural grooves, and you know what they are going to say before they say it. There is no originality and no freshness and no immediacy of response, and therefore there is no seeing.

I think Christians who meditate are self-initiating people, since we no longer have formal rites of passage in our cultures. (See www.malespirituality.org for modern male rites of passage.) Also, the church's sacraments of initiation have been too prettified and clericalized (in my humble opinion!). Over the long haul, faithfulness to contemplative practice can achieve the same radical inner renewal as good sacraments and formal initiation rites.

Contemplation is radical because it is trying to address the root, the underlying place, where illusion and ego are generated. It touches the unconscious where most of our wounds and need for healing lie. With meditation or contemplation, I think we have every likelihood of producing actual elders for the next generation and for the church, and not just elderly people.

Chapter Ten

HOPE THAT IS NO FANTASY

H ope, it seems to me, is the fruit of a learned capacity to suffer wisely and generously. You come out much *larger* and that *largeness* becomes your hope. The ego needs success to thrive, the soul needs only meaning. The Gospel gives human suffering deep, personal, and cosmic meaning, by connecting our pain to the pain of others and, finally, by connecting us to the very "pain of God" for the world. Any form of contemplation is a gradual free fall into such Fullness, or what I have been calling here the Unified Field. There is always a deep, satisfying, truly surprising, and yet certain hope. Logically, I cannot tell you why.

People of such prayer are, frankly, doing themselves a great favor, or, as Jesus says, they get a hundred times more in this life, which bubbles forth into a limitless life, or eternal life (Matt 19:29) later. What a deal! If you have it now, you will have it then. Why would God not give divine union to you later, while giving it so freely, gratuitously, and undeservedly now? Why would God change policies? Lives of inner union, a contemplative life, is simply *practicing for heaven now*. God holds together my contradictions now—why stop holding them later? God allows me to bring "on earth what is in heaven" (Matt 6:10) every time I allow, receive, and forgive the conflicts of the moment and sit in peace and freedom. A life without such contradictions is only half a life, and we are the followers of One who holds together all of the seeming opposites of creation.

Contemplation is no fantasy, no make-believe, no day-dream, but the flowering of patience and steady persever-ance. When we look at the world today, we may well ask whether it can be transformed on the global level. What I have tried to show is that there is a deep relationship between the inner revolution of prayer and the transforma-tion of social structures and social consciousness. It says in the Book of Wisdom that "the multitude of the wise is the salvation of the world" (6:24). Our hope lies in the fact that meditation is going to change the society that you live in, just as it has changed you. In the Center's program "Men as Learners and Elders" (M.A.L.Es; see www.malespirituality. org), we have said modestly and yet ambitiously that we hope our work will have reintroduced, five generations from now, the practice of male initiation in the West. It is that kind of long-term thinking that God seems to be involved in, and kindly invites us into the same patient process.

I know the situation in the world can seem dark today. We see regression—theologically into fundamentalist reli-gion, which thinks that all religious issues can be resolved by an appeal to authority (either hierarchy or Scripture), and so it has no need for an inner life or prayer. It desper-ately doubts and fears inner authority, which, as we said, is the very new covenant that Jesus and Jeremiah promised us. In America, we have seen the rolling back of any compas-sionate economic system, and the abandonment of our bib-lical responsibility for the poor. Fear and anger seem to rule our politics and our churches. You see these same things in many other parts of the world, too. The negative forces are very strong, and the progressive development of conscious-ness and love sometimes feels very weak, but actually it isn't. People like Joanna Macy, David Korten, Ken Wilber, and Thomas Berry speak of "A Great Turning" or "Integral Consciousness," which is indeed happening right below the radar. In that difficult Letter to the Romans, St. Paul has a marvelous line: "*Where sin increased, grace abounded all the more*" (Rom 5:20). That seems to be very true. In country after country, there are so many signs of the Holy Spirit working at all levels of society. The church might well have done much of its work as leaven, which both Jesus and Paul speak of, because much of this reform, enlightenment, compassion, and healing is outside the bounds of organized religion. Like good parents, we want our kids to get the credit. And in the end, we know that only God deserves the credit.

Take, for example, the word *nonviolence*. It didn't exist in the English or German language in the year 1900, because the concept didn't exist. So here we had Jesus who lived a nonviolent life, taught it, and died it, and the world that proceeded from his teaching didn't even understand the concept enough to have a word for it. Now there is enough evolution of consciousness and awareness that we can talk about such things. *Justice* was also not a common word in the Catholic Church I grew up in, nor, as I said, was the idea of healing. The word *healing* was not a household word in many Christian denominations as recent as the 1970s. *Once there is the word, there is the beginnings of consciousness.* And we are the people resulting from the Word that became flesh, and continuing ever-deeper embodiment, even if it still appears a bit below the radar. The seers can see it.

I don't think any pope, any scandals, or any Right- or Left-wing conspiracy can stop it now; the toothpaste is out of the tube, and there are enough people who know the big picture of Jesus' thrilling and alluring vision of the reign of God. There are enough people going on solid inner journeys, and so it is not ideological or theoretical. For the first time on a broad basis, this reformation can come from the inside, and in a positive nonviolent way. This one is not just from the top down, but much more from the bottom up; not from the outside in, but from the inside out. Not from clergy to laity, but from a Unified Field where such class questions are of minor importance. The big questions are being answered at a peaceful and foundational level, with no need to oppose or deny or reject. One almost senses the urgency of the Holy Spirit with six billion of God's creatures now on the planet at the same time. There is so much to still love and embrace and allow to live.

Contemplatives are on the front line for such a reform. Groups like Contemplative Outreach and the World Community for Christian Meditation are, prophetically, ecumenical. I am convinced that the only future of the Christian Church, the one Body of Christ, is ecumenical and shared (Eph 4:1–6). Each of our traditions has preserved and fostered one or the other jewel in the huge crown that is the Cosmic Christ; only together can we make up the unity of the Spirit, as we learn to defer to one another out of love. In contemplative "sits" and prayer, so many of our differences in history, rituals, and languages are of little help or importance now.

If it seems to any of you that I have been overly hard on Catholicism, Christianity, organized religion, or even my country of America, I want to point out that it was these very institutions that gave me the criteria and held me inside the crucible long enough to come back and say these things. It is by our public values, from our documents and Scriptures, and by our own criteria, that I dare to critique anything. If I had not been held inside the crucible of Catholicism, butted up against its inconsistencies and my own inconsistencies, I don't think I would know anything. If I had just wandered around inside my own head, outside of some good containment and guidance from both Scripture and Tradition, I would not dare to speak.

So it seems to me that true progress, or the hope that we have, is not naively optimistic, a straight line, or without regress. Spiritual progress, ironically, develops through tragedy and through falling, where we end up ironically, as C. G. Jung said, "finding pure gold," the gold of the Gospels, and, most surprisingly of all, the hidden gold of our own souls, and the lovely gold of Life Itself. All at the same time. And all as gift.

You might even say at this point, that our "place to stand" becomes our best and biggest "lever" to move the world. Our free fall into Pure Be-ing becomes our very best do-ing.

The Center for Action and Contemplation
Easter Sunday, 2010

FOR FURTHER READING

This list of books that are referred to, even obliquely, in *A Lever and a Place to Stand* does not pretend to be exhaustive or complete. Rather, it is a gathering of titles referred to, as well as other texts that influenced the writing or thinking processes behind this book.

Armstrong, Regis J., OFM CAP, and Ignatius C. Brady, OFM, translators. *Francis and Clare: The Complete Works*. Classics of Western Spirituality. Mahwah, NJ / New York: Paulist Press, 1982.

Barry, Patrick, OSB, translator. *Saint Benedict's Rule*. Mahwah, NJ / New York: HiddenSpring, 2004.

Branick, Vincent P. *Understanding Paul and His Letters*. Mahwah, NJ / New York: Paulist Press, 2009.

De Mello, Anthony. *Awareness: The Perils and Opportunities of Reality*. New York: Image, 1990.

House, Adrian. *Francis of Assisi: A Revolutionary Life*. Mahwah, NJ / New York: HiddenSpring, 2001.

Main, John. *Word into Silence: A Manual for Christian Meditation*. London: Canterbury Press, 2008.

———. *John Main: Essential Writings*. Maryknoll, NY: Orbis, 2008.

———. *The Heart of Creation*. Edited by Laurence Freeman. London: Canterbury Press, 2007.

————. *Monastery without Walls: The Spiritual Letters of John Main*. Edited by Laurence Freeman. London: Canterbury Press, 2006.

————. *Door to Silence: An Anthology for Meditation*. Edited by Laurence Freeman. London: Canterbury Press, 2006.

————. *The Way of Unknowing: Expanding Spiritual Horizons Through Meditation*. Eugene, OR: Wipf and Stock, 2004.

————. *Moment of Christ*. New York: Continuum, 1998.

————. *Silence and Stillness in Every Season: Daily Readings with John Main*. New York: Continuum, 1998.

Martin, James, SJ. *Becoming Who You Are: Insights on the True Self from Thomas Merton and Other Saints*. Mahwah, NJ / New York: HiddenSpring, 2006.

Merton, Thomas. *Selected Poems of Thomas Merton*. Enlarged edition. New York: New Directions, 1967.

Pine-Coffin, R. S., trans. and ed. *Confessions of Saint Augustine*. New York: Penguin, 1961.

Rohr, Richard. *The Naked Now: Learning to See as the Mystics See*. New York: Crossroad, 2009.

————. *Things Hidden: Scripture As Spirituality*. Cincinnati: Saint Anthony Messenger Press, 2008.

————. *From Wild Man to Wise Man: Reflections on Male Spirituality*. Cincinnati: Saint Anthony Messenger Press, 2005.

————. *Simplicity: The Freedom of Letting Go*. New York: Crossroad, 2004.

————. *Everything Belongs: The Gift of Contemplative Prayer*. New York: Crossroad, 1999.

————. *Job and the Mystery of Suffering: Spiritual Reflections*. New York: Crossroad, 1998.

————. *Radical Grace: Daily Meditations*. Edited by John Bookser Feister. Cincinnati: Saint Anthony Messenger Press, 1995.

Rohr, Richard, and Andreas Ebert. *The Enneagram: A Christian Perspective*. New York: Crossroad, 2001.

Rohr, Richard, and Joseph Martos. *The Great Themes of Scripture: New Testament*. Cincinnati: Saint Anthony Messenger Press, 1988.

Rohr, Richard, with John Bookser Feister. *Hope Against Darkness: The Transforming Vision of Saint Francis in an Age of Anxiety*. Cincinnati: Saint Anthony Messenger Press, 2001.

————. *Jesus' Plan for a New World: The Sermon on the Mount*. Cincinnati: Saint Anthony Messenger Press, 1996.

Stourton, Edward. *Paul of Tarsus: A Visionary Life*. Mahwah, NJ / New York: HiddenSpring, 2005.

Walsh, James, ed. *The Cloud of Unknowing*. Classics of Western Spirituality. Mahwah, NJ / New York: Paulist Press, 1982.

green press
INITIATIVE